Disclaimer

The information included in this book is designed to provide helpful information on the subjects discussed. This book is not meant to be used to diagnose or treat any medical condition. For diagnosis or treatment of any medical problem, consult your own doctor. The author and publisher are not responsible for any specific health or allergy needs that may require medical supervision and are not liable for any damages or negative consequences from any application, action, treatment, or preparation, to anyone reading or following the information in this book. Links may change and any references included are provided for informational purposes only.

Facebook Marketing

World Class Strategies for Optimizing Your Page, Getting Lots of Likes, and Creating Compelling Facebook Ads That Produce Powerful Results

By Susan Hollister
Copyright © 2018

Table of Contents

CHAPTER 5: HOW TO USE FACEBOOK LIKE A PRO FOR YOUR BUSINESS 46

CHAPTER 6: CREATING INCREDIBLE FACEBOOK ADS, EVENTS, AND COMPETITIONS 63

CHAPTER 7: CREATING WORLD CLASS CONTENT

CHAPTER 8: THE BEST MARKETING STRATEGIES FOR FACEBOOK..91

Introduction

Perhaps you want to launch a Facebook business page, or maybe you already have tried and are just not seeing the results you were hoping for. Every day hundreds of people begin their own social media journeys, excited about the potential this new form of marketing has to offer to help build their businesses. This may be their first attempt at establishing a Facebook business page; for others, it's a second or even third try. Some people get it right; they increase their revenues quickly, almost effortlessly, harnessing the power of the internet to sell beyond their wildest dreams. However, for most of us, this is not the case. Many of us struggle to make the internet work for us. In many cases, the reason we struggle is because we have little or no understanding of the intricate details and strategies involved that compound over time to make a big difference in the long term. A big mistake many often make is not learning from experts in the field before they start marketing and spending money.

Many of us just launch headfirst into a marketing campaign with no planning or strategy and no clear picture of what we want to achieve. If we're lucky, we get a "like" or "follow" button added to our website, we invite customers and friends to join our Facebook page, and then we begin posting updates. Eventually, however, we realize that all our effort and enthusiasm is having little to no effect on our sales figures. Increased likes and followers rarely morph into increased sales without a clear idea of exactly what it is that we're trying to accomplish.

It's important that we convey our vision to our audience of potential customers the first time they see us in a compelling way. Statistics show that unless our readers are "hooked" the first time, they are unlikely to even return to a site, much less "like" or share it. Too many people continue to plug away, just hoping for a miracle that will transform their Facebook business page into a profitable concern.

Many simply give up when the hoped-for miracle doesn't appear. Others just keep on keeping on, trusting that someday their social media sites will magically begin to work for them, even as they cast about for a solution to their marketing dilemma.

I know exactly how these business owners feel. This is where my personal social media marketing journey began. I knew there *had* to be a trick to using social media to my financial advantage. However, I felt like I was bashing my head against a brick wall time and time again. In my research, I kept pulling up the same information on the internet; it would vaguely say something about engagement and then I would be steered toward another expensive course of one sort or another. Even though I spent an enormous amount of time reading blogs and studying books, nothing pointed me in the right direction to help me progress in the real world of social media marketing.

The turning point came when I stopped just keeping on and made it my aim to explore and ultimately understand everything I could about how businesses make social media sites work for them. I set about studying numerous online marketing campaigns to give me a better idea of what was working and what wasn't. I explored and tried to understand how other people were able to successfully harness the power of Facebook to help their businesses achieve their marketing goals. I was relentless and did not stop until I found answers to my questions. I left no stone unturned when it came to learning about marketing opportunities that could help any type of business, including mine, generate leads and increase revenue.

Now that I've spent more than three years on this quest, I am confident enough to pass on this vital information to you. Through this book, I'm jump-starting your marketing skills. It shouldn't take you as long as it took me to learn how to market a business effectively on Facebook. I can see you using this information to achieve your greatest profits, to reach the right customers, and to nurture a successful business. This is our shared goal.

If you are seriously committed to building your business to its greatest potential and being on the receiving end of some truly incredible results, this book is a must-have. Regardless of whether you are just starting up your business or you are already up and running, this book can help you improve and achieve the greatest success with Facebook marketing.

This book will give you the essential information you need in order to prepare, to plan, and to launch marketing campaigns on Facebook that will help you to generate leads, to find new customers, and ultimately to make more sales.

Social media undoubtedly can make a difference in your profits. Their ongoing development continues to revolutionize the marketplace, enabling you to effectively serve more people than ever before. Their nominal cost and simple accessibility make it easy to overlook the fact that unless you know what you're doing when you tap into the online market, you can waste a lot of effort, not to mention money, while accomplishing nothing significant.

This book, however; is designed to set you up with the very skills and strategies you need to get the most out of social media marketing, especially on Facebook. I'll show you how you can successfully plan, prepare, and launch the perfect Facebook campaign.

You Can Expect to Discover:

- What social media marketing is, why it's essential for any business today, and where businesses tend to go off-course in their marketing campaigns. These three items are important to understand before you start your quest.

- The psychology behind why and how people choose to purchase anything and how you can use this to your advantage in your own marketing campaigns. You don't need a degree in psychology to grasp how this works; just a basic understanding of human nature will do.

- Why and how to define your business, your brand, and your target customer base. This requires a lot of thought on your part, but the results will be well worth your effort.

- How to lay the groundwork for your social media campaigns. The clear guidelines I've provided will help you start off right.

- How to set up a Facebook business page. Using the step-by-step instructions outlined in this book, your Facebook business page will be designed for success.

- How to successfully manage a Facebook campaign. Once your Facebook business campaign is established, it will require tender loving management to become and remain successful.

- How to use recent changes in Facebook to your advantage. You'll be geared up to watch for changes as Facebook makes them. This will not only help you adjust your marketing strategies for greater success but can also ensure that you're not running afoul of any newly-established regulations.

- Step-by-step instructions for establishing your business profile on Facebook. Your business profile is your introduction to your new readers and potential new customers. You will want to present your best face in this introduction.

- The true value of quality marketing content and how to achieve it consistently. Quality marketing content is the heart and soul of your Facebook business page and will determine the number of likes and shares that your page generates. It is hoped that these likes and shares will become repeat customers.

- Practical ways to manage your campaigns and monitor their effectiveness. Once you've launched a marketing campaign on Facebook, I'll help you set up a plan to closely monitor your results, so you can focus your efforts on what brings the greatest results.

- The confidence to establish and maintain a successful Facebook business page.

I have put a great deal of my heart and soul into researching and producing this book; I hope to pass on to you my passion for Facebook marketing so that you will be motivated to use it to make a tangible difference in your business. My hope is that this book will inspire you and help your business flourish as you implement the very strategies that have proven successful for me.

Social media is constantly advancing in technology and changing; therefore, it is vital not to get left behind. Facebook marketing is one of the many recent innovations that is essential to the success of any business. Let's see how it can help yours.

Chapter 1: The Power of Social Media Marketing

In the past 15 years, social media marketing (SMM) has led the revolution on how businesses reach their target markets. It has leveled the playing field for small businesses, because anybody can now reach out to a target market. This form of marketing is easily utilized by businesses of any size; it is a cost-effective, time-saving, and straightforward method of reaching new customers and keeping in contact with an established customer base.

In 2005, The Huffington Post published an article in which it confirmed that more than half of the adult population has a social media profile and is active online, every day. Of all the social media sites out there, Facebook was reported as the most popular among adults (no surprise), with Instagram, Pinterest, LinkedIn, and Twitter all showing strong followings.

Most of the adults I know use social media sites regularly to stay in touch with family and friends. Increasingly, they are using social media to learn about new products available, and a growing number have become completely comfortable with purchasing items online.

Before the computer age, the main ways to communicate outside of face-to-face contact involved using pen and paper or the telephone. Over the past 50 years, the ways we can keep in touch have grown exponentially. The wave of innovation started with the telephone, added the answering machine, and then produced pagers – remember them? – and now portable laptops, tablets, and smartphone apps make instant communication with anyone, anywhere, the norm.

Research shows that no matter how hectic our lives, we thrive on social interaction and social media applications are built to capitalize on these most fundamental needs. We all have the same basic needs:

- To belong – We are wired for community. Messaging groups are a natural result of this desire. Social media users are picky about which sites they frequent.

- To be accepted – That's why Facebook has those emoticons you can tap on to show your approval of someone's message. It marks you as part of a group that accepts a specific opinion. (Be careful about using emoticons - using too many or using them inappropriately can be obnoxious.)

- To be respected – The violation of this social need is apparent online by the advent of cyber bullying. Remember that tone of voice isn't available online. What may be intended to be a joke may not come across that way in a written post. On the other hand, just think how great you feel when somebody "likes" your latest message or post.

- To be loved – Need I say more? Online dating sites continue to proliferate and a growing number of couples first meet online. The expansion of specialty dating sites (farmers, over 50s, etc.) means that more people are accessing these sites with varying degrees of success.

- To have a voice – Not only are your words easily broadcast to the farthest reaches of the world, they're immediately available. Comments and feedback requests are a great example of how this need plays out online.

Whatever You Need, There's an App for That!

Social media outlets wield an enormous impact on our daily lives, both personally and professionally; they not only offer new ways to communicate, but they also allow us to connect and form relationships. We can easily establish connections and stay in touch with old friends; everybody can read as much about our personal information, our feelings, and our experiences as we wish to share. We can have instant access to knowledge about all sorts of things.

The smartphone market continues to grow – most of my friends wouldn't be without one – another example of the importance of instant access to the internet at all times. We now live in a virtual world, which means that we can connect with others at any time and any place, the world over.

While many people use social media to keep in touch, other purposes include:

- Joining a community or group of people who share a specific interest or concern. These communities may be social, political, educational, religious or may encompass any other like-minded group.

- Expressing one's voice and receiving validation for one's feelings and opinions.

- Searching out and reconnecting with old friends. In our mobile society today, it's often difficult to keep in touch with old friends. By using the various search engines available to us, we can locate these old friends and by mutual agreement, re-establish a relationship.

- Sharing personal news. What quicker way to announce to a large group important information such as an engagement, a new baby (complete with photos!), or a promotion?

- Researching product information. Using the internet, you can research information about the performance, reliability, and cost of just about anything, from refrigerators to new cars. No more buying a pig in a poke!

- Establishing a relationship with a service provider. Having trouble getting through to your doctor's office to make an appointment? Access his website and do it online! Book a time for your car's oil change, or make a dinner reservation, all without leaving your recliner!

- Following brands and products of interest. About that dinner reservation - why not try that new bistro that everyone is talking about? You can check out their menu online in advance to see if they offer your favorite French dish - frog legs.

- Local, national, and international news and current affairs updates. Who is ahead in your local race for school board president? What's the latest timetable for troop withdrawal in Afghanistan? Learn all this and more by accessing pertinent online sites.

- Receiving inspiration and motivation. Need a kick in the pants to start writing your Great American Novel or just to clean the bathroom? Check out the various online sites available to inspire and motivate you.

- Launching, advertising, and growing a business. Review all the new entries of businesses that offer what you are interested in. You can be sure that you'll learn something interesting and helpful to you as you set up your own business page.

Once you understand why people are so attached to social media, you will see how important it is for your business to use Facebook wisely to connect with, engage, establish, expand, and sustain your customer base.

To succeed in business, you must first understand just how powerful social media can be. The individuals who aren't connected to the outside world via social media are in the minority. Everybody I know is on Facebook daily. No matter where you go, you will see people with their heads down, engrossed in accessing some type of device, and you can bet they are checking out some type of media site, such as:

- Facebook

- Twitter

- LinkedIn

- Instagram

- Snapchat

The rate at which social media outlets are growing is rapid, making us all part of the social media revolution. Your potential customers are accessing one or more social media sites regularly. Social media connections are increasing at a rapid rate; just type "social media statistics" into Google and you will be astounded, as the figures are in the billions. Facebook alone has more than one billion members (yes, that's right - one BILLION), of whom 95 percent access the site at least once a day.

Online Marketing

In the past, promoting a business was a lonely task, mostly undertaken with a staff of one - you. You might have had the best idea in the world, but unless you had the financing to fund direct mail or magazine advertising, your idea would remain just that, a good idea. Today, however, social media marketing gives business owners virtually limitless opportunities to connect with their target audience, to interact individually with potential new customers, and to even venture into new markets. Today, all businesses, whether large or small, have the same opportunities to attract new customers. If you can learn to use the internet to your advantage, you may just pull ahead of your competition.

Social media marketing is still a relatively new phenomenon. It incorporates all the strategies, processes, and tactics that are used online to gain the attention of potential customers and thus increase revenues. The larger businesses are already capitalizing on our natural desire to connect with others. The beauty of the internet, however, is that size doesn't have any advantage. Even the smallest business has access to everything the internet can offer.

You will find Facebook marketing useful to:

- Pursue and engage with people. Search sites with members who have interests pertinent to your business make for a ready-made target audience.

- Encourage repeat customers and build brand loyalty. Offer specials and incentives to repeat customers to your site.

- Build trust and pique interest in your products and services. Offer something with your product or service that no other similar site is offering.

- Provide information to a specifically targeted market. Zero in on your targeted audience and give them something especially for them, something that no other site gives them.

- Motivate your target audience to share your information with their online friends. Provide incentive for your target audience to share your site information with their friends, whether it be a free e-book, a webinar, or some other "freebie."

All social media campaigns have the same basic goals; they focus their content toward a specific audience with the primary aim of seeing it shared and liked, producing a reaction, and generating comments. Once a business has accomplished these goals, the content will be passed to others via word-of-mouth, which is still the most powerful form of advertising.

Buyers' Behavioral Patterns

The most successful marketers capitalize on the innate need of people to connect with others by various means. They know what motivates people to buy specific products and services and they have applied this knowledge to their own social media campaigns to maximize their profits.

It is vital for businesses to understand and know as much as possible about their customers so that they can market their services/products to their target audience in the most efficient and effective way. Understanding how and why customers make their purchases will help you decide how social media marketing can best work for your business.

Many common elements work together to influence people when they are selecting their purchases. Businesses that know how to incorporate all of these elements into their Facebook campaigns are most destined to be highly successful.

Like Me

There is no denying it, the "like" factor is huge in online marketing. Beyond mastering the psychology behind a person's choosing to buy a product, the "likability factor" is key. Obviously, people are far more inclined to purchase products from a business they know and trust. The most powerful advertising tool remains word-of-mouth promotion. Social media platforms, especially Facebook, have taken this to an entirely new level with the use of the "like" button. Your brand or business name can now be seen by thousands, instantaneously with just one click of the mouse; it only takes a single person who likes your business to get the ball rolling.

Why Market My Business Online?

The short answer: that's where the customers are. Approximately 96 percent of American adults shop online at least once a year; 80 percent shop online monthly, and more than half shop weekly.

Americans shop online for an average of five hours a week, spending almost half of their shopping budget online. Businesses that develop a loyal online following have a distinct advantage in this area.

Although virtually everyone shops online, fewer than half of all American businesses have a website. This is simply amazing, since it's so cheap and easy (often free) to develop one. Tapping into the online marketplace automatically gives you a huge advantage over the majority of your competition.

The ecommerce market continues to expand dramatically; so far, it shows no signs of peaking. If you get involved now, you'll be able to grow along with it, enjoying all the success it can give you.

How is this form of marketing different from the more conventional methods, and why is it so vital for your business? Simply put, social media marketing is more dynamic, efficient, and productive than all the conventional methods combined.

Customers today are increasingly suspicious of traditional marketing; they are far smarter when it comes to making purchases. How often, when you're watching television, do you flip to another channel to avoid sitting through another boring, repetitive television commercial? Customers want a product that is tried, tested and true; they expect to see testimonials and reviews that attest to its effectiveness before they make a purchase. Social media sites specialize in person-to-person interaction in a way that is impossible with traditional marketing media.

Social media marketing wins over traditional marketing in many ways:

- It gives you multiple ways to reach your target audience. You have access to many sites, in addition to backlinking (more about that later) to reach your target audience.

  Never before in history has it been so easy to identify and initially communicate and establish a relationship with your target audience. Using the information that social media sites store about their users, it is easier than ever before for you to specifically tailor your message to reach the key individuals who are most likely to buy your products.

- Social media platforms give businesses direct and immediate contact with their customers. You no longer must wait for the mail or newspaper to be delivered or for a specific television advertising time to be aired to get your information in front of your target audience.

Now you can communicate and stay in touch with your customers on a level that traditional marketing methods have never been able to achieve. With a Facebook business page, you can follow up with a thank you to your customers immediately after they have made a purchase, provide any additional support, and send carefully timed offers that can entice them back for more. You can serve each customer individually, addressing specific needs personally on a one-to-one basis. No longer will customers have to wait days to resolve problems. With online communications, you can provide your customers with immediate responses to their questions and resolutions to their problems.

- Social media marketing harnesses the power of peer recommendation.

Social media marketing makes the most of word-of-mouth endorsements by encouraging consumers to converse, share, and otherwise interact with each other. These sites are designed to encourage the championing and recommendation of products. They make it easy by making available "follow" and "like" buttons in their basic architecture. These buttons allow people to register their opinions without the hassle of writing out a lengthy explanation (although the "comment" feature is readily accessed when needed). Users like the accessibility of expressing an opinion with the click of a mouse.

- Social media marketing helps to build brand awareness.

  The most valuable asset of your business is your brand. It serves as your unique calling card. Social media platforms make it easy for you to identify your target audience, promote brand awareness and encourage brand loyalty. When a consumer chooses to like your Facebook page, it boosts the credibility of your brand to all his or her friends.

- Social media marketing infuses your brand with humanity.

  Facebook allows you to communicate directly with your audience on a personal one-to-one level, infusing your brand with your own personality. People are always more interested in establishing a relationship with a live person than with a faceless corporate drone or worse, a computer. Social media platforms allow you to interact directly with the people who make your business successful, your customers.

- Social media marketing provides continuous exposure for your business.

  Now you can easily connect with both existing and potential customers. You can reach out to them every day if you want and it won't put much of a dent in your budget, either. Research has revealed that on average, people need to interact with a business seven times before they will make a purchase. Under traditional marketing methods this would be time-consuming and expensive, but it is easy and inexpensive to accomplish when you tap into social media.

- Consumer-powered interest is to your advantage.

  Unlike with traditional marketing methods, online customers are exposed to your business by their own choice; they can opt out whenever they wish. They are not inundated with unwanted junk mail or blasting television ads. This means that the people who visit your site want to be there; they have already made the choice to listen to you, so go ahead and boldly address their needs.

- Continuous engagement is an option.

  Social media outlets provide a business with an ongoing dialogue with their audience like no other medium can. Followers who have interacted with a business on the internet are more likely to visit again or visit an online store.

- Experience exponential growth on a viral scale.

  Once followers choose to share your content, it is then seen by their whole network of friends, who are exposed to your business and who, it is hoped, will share with their friends. This can be the start of viral exposure, resulting in a tremendous wave of brand awareness and increased audience numbers, greater sales and a fresh round of exposure as customers in turn share their success stories in dealing with your business.

- Social media sites are business assets.

  Unlike other types of advertising where you can watch your marketing investment disappear and you rarely see direct results, your Facebook business page becomes a valuable business asset that only grows in value over time. If you manage this asset correctly, your network of friends will continue to grow, leading to a steady growth in potential customers and ultimately sales.

- You have complete control over your broadcast channels.

  Unlike traditional broadcast media, with expensive fees and pre-determined and limited air times, your audio and video messages can be aired at any time, on demand, by your customers. Because they only air when requested by a consumer, you won't be pestering individuals with unwanted advertising; instead, you will be communicating directly to the very individuals who want to hear from you, at a time that they're ready to listen.

Once your broadcasts are developed and your following is growing, your business will have the advantage of literally having its own broadcast channel where it can communicate anything 24 hours a day, seven days a week. This advantage cannot be taken away unless you run it incorrectly and lose your followers. As long as you produce content that is pertinent, useful, and interesting, your followers will keep returning to see what you have to report, and they will remain open and willing to purchase additional products from you.

These are just a few of the ways that social media marketing excels over traditional marketing. If you spend any time at all on the internet, you have been subjected to this type of marketing and may not have been aware of it. This form of advertising takes the most advantage of the principle of giving something away in order to win customer loyalty; it's so inexpensive to offer a free e-book or webinar or to provide valuable information on a blog post, that almost everybody with a business website is taking advantage of this simple method to gain loyal subscribers and, ultimately, devoted customers. We'll talk about details later. For now, just remember that this kind of marketing is well within your reach.

Why Facebook?

When it comes to product and service recommendations, Facebook's popularity far outstrips other social media platforms. But why is it so powerful?

It all started when Mark Zuckerberg launched Facebook on the campus of Harvard University in 2004. At first, only students could use the site, but in 2006, after only two years of operation,

Facebook was made accessible to anybody with a computer. Facebook's original "fan pages" morphed over time into today's business pages. Business pages are sites that represent a specific business or brand, extending the business' presence into a whole new universe of potential customers. At this writing, Facebook has nearly two billion (again that's BILLION) active users and is the top social media platform chosen by businesses.

When people see their friends liking a service or product, the likability factor shoots sky high, along with trust and curiosity. People immediately want to see what is so great about this product or service their friends are touting with such enthusiasm. In this environment, a like or a positive comment amounts to a recommendation; that alone can be enough to motivate people to buy or at least to start to follow your business. Now do you see why I think Facebook marketing is so essential to your brand's success?

Chapter 2: How to Get It Right with Facebook

On the face of it, social media marketing is mostly free. However, it takes a sizeable amount of effort to learn how to make the most of this free tool. Of course, that's why this book is so necessary.

Although most business owners have heard about the powerful effectiveness of social media marketing, few are confident of using it to benefit their businesses. Facebook is not designed to automatically lead you down the path of profitability. No, you need to discover that knowledge yourself. I can help you understand what to post and how to post it in order to move your fans to buy your products. Along the line, you'll learn some key skills that will help your business gain traction in the marketplace.

Here are some of the basic skills we'll be talking about in the chapters to come:

- Complete and long-term commitment to Facebook marketing.

  The more you understand about how social media marketing works, the easier it will be to commit to using it over the long haul. And this is a long-term commitment; you don't immediately arrive with a fully developed Facebook marketing campaign, replete with a page that has a huge and vocal following that draws in and converts customers. It's a continual process, involving ongoing self-education.

  You'll be actively tweaking your marketing approach to stay current with trends and to take advantage of current events. The Facebook application itself is continually evolving, adding functionality that a savvy marketer can take advantage of to keep one's business on the cutting edge of success.

- Understand how social media marketing works.

  You'll want to learn how basic marketing principles apply to social media marketing. You'll be discovering how you can implement effective strategies to build a successful Facebook marketing campaign. This goes far beyond just setting up a profile, presenting product images with attractive descriptions, and just hoping people find your new site. You'll be discovering some specific strategies used by successful Facebook marketers and learning how to apply them to your business situation.

- Learn how to turn fans and followers into customers.

  Regardless of how many followers or fans a business has, it doesn't automatically translate into sales. You'll be discovering skills that will help you transform interested individuals into loyal customers.

- Understanding the psychology behind buyer behavior.

  You'll need to learn what lies behind a customer's decision to buy a product or service. Armed with this knowledge, you can more easily design effective marketing campaigns on Facebook.

- Set clear goals for marketing on Facebook.

  As you gain a clear image of what can be accomplished through social media marketing, you will be able to establish specific objectives for what you want to see happen and design practical marketing strategies to get you there.

- Learn to capture and convert leads.

  Discover what leads look like on Facebook and how you can trap and develop them into paying customers.

- Establish reasonable expectations.

  Discover what Facebook can and cannot do for you. Learn how to incorporate Facebook marketing activities in to your daily routine, as well as your future planning activities.

- Learn how to attract the right audience.

  With any business, your marketing plan involves knowing your target audience and how to reach it. If you know these basic principles, you still need to learn how to apply them to the medium of Facebook.

- Know how to get a bigger audience.

  Most businesses need a sizeable audience to make any type of impact. Although engagement is important, engagement comes from your pool of followers. You'll need to know how to increase the size of this pool, to boost the amount of engagement.

- Learn to function proactively.

  You can't just assume that visitors to your site will press the "like" or "follow" button. Unfortunately, this rarely happens. Learn how to give your visitors a good reason to follow your business.

- Learn what to promote.

  Social media marketing is not about pushing products. It's about developing trust. Learn how to shift your focus to trust-building and you'll end up selling more products in the end.

- Learn how to post effectively.

This can be a little tricky. If you post too frequently you'll be classified as spam or as annoying. If you post too seldom, you'll not be seen at all. You also need to know what kind of content is most helpful to post and what to stay away from.

Chapter 3: Setting Up Your Business Page Like A Pro

Creating a Facebook business page is easy. Within a handful of minutes, you can have an attractive page set up, all by yourself. If you have a personal account, you'll have no trouble working with your business page as the principles are very similar.

Here's the general process, step by step:

Step 1: Log into your account

Once you have logged in, you will see your news feed. There will be a tool panel to the left of your screen with a variety of shortcuts. While some of the shortcuts are hidden, you will find the "pages" icon under the "explore" tab. As of the writing of this book, the pages icon is a yellow flag in a small white box next to the word "pages." When you select this link, it will take you to the section for your Facebook pages. Alternatively, you can also type http://www.facebook.com/pages into your web browser to access this page.

Step 2: The homepage

On the homepage for your pages, you will automatically see a list of the existing pages that you've previously "liked." If you look to the upper right-hand corner of this page you will see the words "Create Page." Click on this link and you will be able to choose the kind of page you want to build.

Step 3: Type of Page

In reviewing these page types, you will want to select the one that best describes your business. Of these choices, you will likely select a local business, a large-scale business, or an individual product or brand. Based on your choice, Facebook will then guide you to fill in some additional information.

With a local business, you will be asked for:

- The page name, which will probably be the same as your business name.

- The page category.

  - For example, if you own and run Molly's Sewing Emporium, the category you are most likely to choose will be sewing and materials, clothes making, and the like.

  - Choose the page category for your business most carefully. This can impact the effectiveness of your Facebook business marketing. Amazon's search algorithm relies in large part on your site's category.

- The address and other contact information.

For a **large company** page, you will be asked to choose a descriptive category from a dropdown dialog box and to enter your company name.

For an **individual brand** or product, you will be asked to select a category that your brand or product best fits into and to enter its name.

Step 4: Get started

Once you enter the information Facebook has asked for and click on the "get started" link, Facebook will open the Page Manager. Congratulations, you have officially created your business page!

Navigating Page Manager Menus

Again, you will see different options to your left in the Page Manager. You can choose from:

- **Home**: The home screen is where you will see what your page looks like to other users; you will also see a few extra buttons and features. This is where you should add a picture for your profile as well as a cover picture. Your **profile picture** is what will represent your page the most because it is literally the "face" of your page. Your **cover photo** is equally important because its large size is perfect for capturing attention. I will go into greater detail on the importance of these two items in a couple of chapters.

  This is where you will post status updates. Status updates may consist of text, a picture, a video, or any combination of these items. Use this for announcing discounts and other promotions, or just to stay in touch.

  In the right-hand corner, under your cover photo, you will see an option to "add a button." By clicking on this button, you can create and add a call-to-action button on your page. It can be anything from a "learn more" link to a "sign up" form to a "contact us" option.

- **Posts:** This screen is a second location – in addition to the home page – where you can post a status update and manage all your past posts.

- **Reviews:** Use this area to monitor, respond to, and otherwise manage the reviews customers leave about your business.

- **Videos:** Use this area to add, view, and perform maintenance on your posted videos. The most important feature of this section is the **video insights** button, which lets you see how and when visitors are interacting with your videos. It measures how many views per video you've received as well as how many seconds people have spent viewing each video.

  You can use this to adjust your marketing. For example, if people are only watching the first 30 seconds of your videos, you will be able make changes to capture their attention more quickly, within the first few seconds. The video insights tool will also point out your highest-performing videos, so you can see what you are doing right.

- **Photos**: In this section, you can review and manage all the photos you've uploaded to your page.

- **About:** This is where you'll place key information about your business.

- **Likes:** In this area, you can invite others to "like" your page and you can also find information on how viewers are engaging with it. This is where you'll review how many users are talking about your page and read what they're saying. You can compare the number of "likes" you receive across multiple weeks. This section also lets you see what percentage of viewers liked or followed your page.

- **Groups:** The groups function allows you to link a Facebook group to your business page where you and your audience can interact.

Navigating Page Manager Tabs

These tabs will let you manage the following aspects of your page:

- **Messages:** This tab will take you to your business messenger, the business counterpart of your personal messenger. At the bottom of the business messenger, you will see an option to turn on an "away" feature, which you should activate to let participants know when you've stepped away from managing the page. You can keep the away feature turned on for up to 12 hours.

- **Notifications:** This tab shows all the notifications related to your business page. They are all shown together but can easily be filtered by category.

- **Insights**: This is the heart of business page management. The default view will show you a summary of all the activity generated on your page over the course of the past week. You can look at data regarding page actions, page views, page likes, how many people reached by a specific post, the level of engagement for a post, and the number of video views and page followers. The vast amount information it provides can be used to tweak your marketing strategies for greater efficiency, effectiveness and broader reach.

- **Publishing Tools:** The publishing tools feature allows you to do several things. The default view will display all your published posts along with statistics on how many viewers each one reached and how many engagements they received. It shows when you published each individual post. A search area lets you filter all your published posts by keywords.

The left-side of the screen offers additional options. The next option is "scheduled posts." This is a post you write but choose not to publish it right away. Instead, you choose a specific future date when you want it to be published.

To **schedule** a post for future release, after you've created the post click the "schedule" button. You will notice a drop-down arrow next to the schedule button. This lets you set a specific release date. You can also save your work as an unpublished draft, waiting for further editing or to release whenever you feel like it.

At the same time that you schedule a post to hit the web, you can also set an **expiration date**. This is the time you want the post to stop appearing on your Facebook business page. This option is useful for managing time-sensitive posts, special sales events, or messages that apply to a specific time of year, season, or holiday.

Beneath the scheduled posts option, you'll see the word "Drafts." By clicking on this tab, you will see all the posts you have worked on but have not yet published.

"**Expired posts**" are those that have reached their designated expiration date and have been removed from circulation on your Facebook business page.

- **Videos** have their own section. You can view your established collection and upload your latest videos by clicking on "Video Library." There is also an option to post a live video, which is a feed that you stream in real time.

Underneath "Video Library," you will see "Videos You Can Cross-post." This is a slick feature that allows you to team up with another Facebook business page to cross-post each other's published videos. This is helpful for expanding your reach to new potential customers.

To sign up for this feature, go to your page settings, look on the left side of the screen to select the "cross-posting" option. Then type in a Facebook business page you want to link to. The individual in charge of this other page must approve the request. Once your request is accepted, you can then begin to cross-post videos. Whenever you upload a video, you will be prompted to select the option to cross-post and can then select the specific page you want it to appear on.

- Beneath the video options you will notice another section called "**Lead Ad Forms**." Lead ads are Facebook advertisements that allow your customers to give you their personal information when they want to know more about your product or service. You can then use that information to reach out to the potential customer and develop the relationship from there.

For example, your lead ad could ask your customers for their email address in exchange for a free newsletter or e-book. If your customers are interested in receiving your newsletter or free e-book, they will provide you with their email addresses, which you should add to your list of contacts for future online communication. The generic contact forms will already be put together when you create a lead ad on Facebook. You will have the option to customize the questions you ask on each form.

One of the best features that Facebook provides to their business page owners is to the ability to download new leads generated by your business page. You can save them to your device or transfer them directly into a customer relationship management program. Since Facebook owns Instagram, a site that primarily focuses on photo-sharing, you can integrate lead ad forms into your Instagram account.

"Lead Ad Forms" gives you the ability to download and archive active contact forms generated within the past 90 days. Facebook deletes lead ad forms every 90 days, so it behooves you to download contact forms on a regular basis. An option below "Lead Ad Forms" allows you to view form drafts that have not yet been published.

Chapter 4: The Best Strategies For Search Engine Optimization

Search engine optimization, or SEO, is a tactic used to boost the visibility of your website by labeling it with the important keywords in your business page that are popular with search engines. Search engine optimization will result in increased online traffic, which essentially leads to greater exposure of your site and, ultimately, to more sales. Sites that have a lot of high-quality content (i.e., text densely populated with specific keywords) can rank high without using any special techniques. However, it can take a very long time for a website to rise to prime positioning at the top of search results. SEO is how you reach that coveted spot for your business page.

Keyword Selection

Keywords are, well, key to optimizing your visibility in the eye of search engines. They consist of specific words that most closely describe the topic of your website or an individual post. You want to tune in to and focus on words that best reflect the identity of your business. For example, a nutritional business may have as its main keyword the term "nutrition," with secondary keywords of "healthy eating," "food science," and "health." Search engine software will read and analyze your page to discern if its content is rife with repeated keywords. It looks for keywords in critical areas such as the website's title, headers, metatags, and in the text of a post. It is important to use keywords that fit into your content naturally, without looking as if the keywords were simply forced into the site. If you stuff your text with keywords at random or insert keywords too close together to read naturally, the search engine may arbitrarily decide that you're trying to trick the system and it'll refuse to rank your page (clever little search engine!).

Metatags

Metatags are tags placed within the lead section of your site description. They help to define the contents of your web page. For example, internet search engines may include a brief description of your page in their search results. This description will enable your potential customers to see at a glance that your site contains information important to them.

The most important metatags for search engine optimization are the *keywords* metatag and the *description* metatag. The keywords metatag looks for the words or phrases that best describe the contents of the page. In addition to looking for keywords, the description metatag also includes a brief one- or two-sentence description of the page. Both the keywords and the description metatags are used by search engines to determine where to add a page to their index. Some search engines also use the description metatag to show a searcher a summary of the business page's contents.

Although most search engines also use the contents of a page to determine where and how to list a business on its index page, the creator of a web page should be sure to include metatags with both appropriate keywords and description. Well-chosen and well written metatags can help make your business page rank higher in search results.

Backlinking

The second component of SEO is backlinking. Let's imagine that some people are discussing nutrition in an online forum and one of the users provides a link to your website: this is called backlinking. Backlinking is when other websites link to yours, allowing their visitors to also visit your site. Search engine software knows how to detect that as well. When it sees that many websites link back to yours, your backlinking score will be higher and your website is more likely to rank higher in search results. However, the websites linking to your site must also have high-quality content for the search engine to boost your ranking. One technique some website owners try is to swap links with other websites to boost their backlinking score. However, backlinking must be relevant. For example, if a website about race cars backlinks to your website about nutrition, the search engine will know it's irrelevant and will not let this link boost your page ranking. And talking about a certain brand of gasoline as nutrition for your car doesn't meet the criteria! Again, this is in place to prevent website owners from trying to game the system.

If you look hard enough you can discover the techniques some people use to try to scam the search engine optimization system, but trying these techniques is only a waste of time, since most search engines are highly programmed to be able to detect what you're doing. Trying to trick, cheat, or scam the system is known as **black hat SEO** and your best bet is to avoid it altogether. Why risk drawing unwanted attention from the search engine algorithms and missing out on attracting many new potential customers? If you're using these tactics, then it's probably a sign that customers will think your website isn't worth visiting in the end anyway. The best strategy is to find a balance of keyword use and backlinking to supplement your engaging use of quality text, photos, videos, games or anything else you can think of that will satisfy both your customers and the search engine software. Adhering to this practice will show your customers that you're committed to providing them with high-quality content. This will result in their increased participation, which will also catch the all-seeing eye of the search engine.

Since all business pages are available for public view, your information is right there just waiting to be analyzed by major search engines. Although Facebook pages are different from original websites in that you can only build your Facebook business page from a template, as opposed to writing your own code to define it, there are still many ethical ways you can help your Facebook page rank high in results generated by the various search engines.

Optimizing Your Page Name

Your **page name** is the first item to address. This is what you want your potential customers to see first. The most important place to put your main keyword is in the first word of your name.

If you are a nutritional expert who provides tips on healthy eating, your optimized page name could be something like "Nutritionist John Smith." You want your name to convey the idea of what your site will provide. Why is it so important to put your main keyword in the beginning of your name? Think of it this way: if you do an internet search for John Smith nutritionist, the search engine you use will bring you all the results for all entries for "John Smith" first, regardless of who they are or what they do. However, if you type in "nutritionist John Smith," the search engine is more likely to bring you results relevant to nutritionists named John Smith and that's what you were looking for to begin with.

Give yourself enough time to come up with a page name that conveys as closely as possible what your website will offer new customers. Although Facebook will let you change your page name a certain number of times, once you've chosen your name, stick with it. If you've chosen carefully, there should be no need to change it. Because search engines will index everything on the page under the page name, changing this essential piece of information may cost you in search visibility and possible customers.

Once you've chosen your perfect business page name, you will want to sprinkle your main keyword throughout your page, paying particular attention to the company overview section and the "about" area. Optimize your business page's short description as well; it's one of the first things your visitors will see.

Optimizing Your Custom URL

When you create a business page on Facebook, you will be given a URL that states your page name, followed by some numbers that are unique to your business. This initial URL is long, unattractive and difficult to remember. However, Facebook will allow you to create a custom URL once your page receives 25 likes. You will want to use this feature to your advantage! You won't be allowed to change your custom URL once you've picked it so choose it wisely. If possible, it should exactly match or at least come close to the URL of your actual website.

To customize your URL, you will create your "username," as Facebook calls it. Select this option and type in what you want your custom URL to be. Following the example above, your Facebook page link with a custom URL would look something like this: www.facebook.com/NutritionistJohnSmith.

Don't limit yourself to using only one keyword but also don't make an extensive, exhausting list either. Choose four to five important keywords that your potential customers are most likely to use to find businesses such as yours. For example, a great custom URL could be www.facebook.com/FreeNutritionTips, if part of what you're offering is free nutrition tips. Keep your custom URL short so that it is memorable, so people are less likely to forget it.

Optimizing Posts

You can optimize your **status updates** using the same strategies I discussed above. Every time you post a text update, integrate your keywords as best and as naturally as you can, preferably within the first 18 characters. Facebook arbitrarily uses these characters as part of a post's metatag, so you'll want to maximize keyword presence here. It can be a challenge to make your status sound as natural as possible while still including the keywords, but the effort will definitely be worth it. As you did with your business page name, try to put the most important keywords as close to the beginning as possible.

Whenever you upload a picture or a video, you can write a description to accompany it. You'll want to include your keywords here as well, in the most natural way possible. You'll also want to add a backlink directly to your company website at the end of each status update, as long as it fits naturally. You can copy and paste the link to your website directly into the status update. This sets you up for backlinking, as I described earlier in this chapter; more on how to backlink in a bit.

Post, Post, Post!

The next step is to post as much high-quality content as often as you can! I will get more into what constitutes high-quality content in a few chapters. If you don't post to your page, visitors cannot see, like, or share your content, your page will be useless, and your business will suffer. Don't worry — posting often doesn't mean that you'll need to be in front of your computer or mobile device all day. Many companies hire an employee to manage their social media pages. However, even if you can't hire someone to optimize your posts, you can find automated programs that will do the work for you. I will describe these programs in greater detail a little later.

Don't forget to fill in the details about your location when you're filling in your business page information, especially if you're a brick-and-mortar business. This helps your page rank higher in search engine results when customers type your business in along with a location. Also include your phone number and hours of operation.

Even if your address is unimportant to sales, you should use the products box to provide targeted keywords. Not only is all of this information crucial for bringing your customers to your business site, but search engines also tend to rank pages with detailed information higher in searches.

Facebook Notes are an effective, but highly underutilized, tool for search engine optimization. When you post a status under your business page, Facebook will allow you to choose "write a note." The most important pieces of a note are the title and the announcement that Facebook posts to your page once you publish it (*Nutritionist John Smith* published a note titled *Handy Hacks for Healthy Eating*). You can write a note about anything related to your business and of course sprinkle in some keywords in a natural manner if you can.

More about Backlinking

As mentioned earlier, Backlinking is critical to search engine optimization so I will provide a bit of additional context here

As I described earlier, backlinks are links referring your audience to another site. The more high-quality backlinks your page has, the better your chances are of showing up at the top of search engine results. If your backlinks are of low quality, they will probably not help your ranking. For a backlink to be considered of high quality, it must come from a relevant website that has its own high-quality content and visitors must access it often. The anchor text should ideally match at least one of your keywords, and the link should ideally be included within the content and be located high on the page and not off to the side. It should be as organic as possible. The best possible scenario is when a website decides to link to your page on its own. It's also ideal if the website backlinking to your page isn't littered with other backlinks, but the few that it does have are also of high-quality.

For a backlink to work properly, it must be a clickable hyperlink and not just copied and pasted text. You can insert a hyperlink into regular text. The text that serves as the base for the hyperlink is called **anchor text**. When you insert a hyperlink into anchor text, the text becomes clickable and will take you to the destination of the link attached to it.

Although your page will obtain organic backlinks over time, you can attempt to build backlinks yourself by reaching out to other relevant established websites and social media pages. You should think of building backlinks as a form of networking. While exchanging links with other sites will not hurt your ranking, search engines usually assume that the backlink is of high quality, particularly if your site has no backlink to the site that is linking with you.

Also, it is important to use backlinking sources that are related to your business – otherwise the search engine is likely to mark it as spamming, making it a waste of your time.

Backlink consistently. If you set up a high number of backlinks within a few days and then stop all activity, the search engines will decide that you're trying to trick the system.

Since building backlinks, the right way can take time, there are services available that will build backlinks for you. Take the time to research any service owners before you commit to them. You will want to be confident that they can provide you with high quality, relevant backlinks. You'll also want to research the average cost for a backlinking service in your field of interest. Costs will definitely vary. Beware of backlinking services that offer their services at an outrageously low price. As they say, "If it looks too good to be true, it probably is. "

The best way to entice a website to organically link back to your page is to provide unique and engaging content that other people will find interesting. Facebook business pages are unique in that you can host contests and write notes or post special content that otherwise wouldn't be effective on your main website. Take advantage of the features that Facebook business pages offer and use them to give other websites a good reason to backlink to you!

If your main website has a blog, there is one awesome backlinking strategy you can try: copy each of your blog entries into separate Facebook notes. This is a win-win strategy because you are providing high quality content to your existing visitors and if someone who runs another website thinks your content is interesting or informative and important, there is a higher chance they will backlink to your Facebook note instead of your actual blog.

Remember, search engines are smart - don't try to scam the system!

Chapter 5: How To Use Facebook Like A Pro For Your Business

Optimizing Content

Content refers to everything you post on your business page for your followers to see. Many businesses post photos and videos as well as text, since these are the most popular forms of content. Content can make or break a page. You'll need to know what to use and how to most effectively represent it as content.

There are four key tips to remember when choosing the best content:

1. The content of your business page must be relevant and reflect what your business does and the values it upholds.

2. Your content must be consistent in quality and style, regardless of the medium you use. Consumers put a high value on consistency and have come to expect the highest level of quality in the sites they visit. Your standards must be very high indeed.

3. Your content must motivate customers to engage with your business, going from first-time visitor, to regular reader, to loyal repeat customer.

4. Your content needs to appeal to your target audience, making them want to participate as a regular reader of your posts. First, you need to determine what you have done to encourage readers to like your page. Then you'll want to provide them with high-quality target information that applies to those interests.

Do people like your page because you provide discount codes? Do they value the practical usefulness of the information you share? Regardless of the reason, consumers must receive something that they value in exchange for their participation on your Facebook business page. Find out what your target audience values and then work out ways to deliver it in the form of high-quality content.

Posts that are purely text can be incredibly powerful. Because of this, Facebook has launched an option where you post short text using a large font on colorful backgrounds. The larger-than-usual text, on top of vibrant colors and patterns, stands out above the normal chatter on a page.

The most powerful content for any Facebook business page are videos and photos. Adding these to your posts will not just make your post stand out but it will also make your post more shareable. The more your posts are shared, the larger will be your audience and the greater your potential income

Using Images

Posts that include photos are 20 percent more likely to create engagement than posts without images. If posts include a video, the likelihood of engagement jumps to 80 percent.

When you use pictures and videos on your Facebook business page, they must be of the best quality and the highest resolution. Decent quality content marks you as a professional and it will make your readers more likely to share your content than will images that are blurry or text riddled with typos.

You'll want to carefully select pictures for use in your **profile**, your **cover photo,** and your **timeline**. Facebook promotes and supports the use of three types of picture files:

- .png

- .jpg

- .gif

Pictures that you have taken using a camera are best saved in a .jpg format. Graphics that are computer-generated, such as your business logo, are best saved in .png or .gif format. When you add a picture to your business page, Facebook will compress it, so no matter how large the file, it will not slow down the speed at which your page loads. Because of this compression, it is important that you save your pictures in the highest resolution available to you. If you use low resolution images, the compression will cause them to appear grainy and of poor quality, a turn-off to your potential customers.

Your Cover Image

Your **cover photo** can have a full display size of 820x312 pixels with a minimum of 399x150 pixels. Facebook allows you to upload a single cover photo. When you are ready to upload your cover photo, simply click the camera button you'll find on the bottom right-hand side of your top banner. Since your cover photo consists of a single image, it's vital that you are creative to maximize this important advertising medium. Collages can be useful. I suggest you create your cover image outside of Facebook by combining several shots of your business into a single image, then uploading this image. This will give you the ability to play around with the format, making changes until you are satisfied with its appearance.

While your cover photo can only be a single image, you can change it out as often as you like. This image is the first impression your target audience get of your business, so it is important to create a memorable impression. You want to use a photo that sums up what your business is about and what your brand represents. You may want to create several photos so that you'll have a replacement handy whenever you're ready for a change. On your cover photo, you'll also want to highlight any upcoming special events or deals you may have running. If you are a dress designer with a newly launched line of wedding dresses, you might display your latest designs in your cover photo.

Facebook has also made it possible for businesses to replace their cover photos with a **cover video**. A high-quality short video can boost your following and may keep you ahead of your competition. As with your cover photo, cover videos must be 820x312 pixels and they should be more than 20 seconds long but no longer than a minute and a half. Once you have uploaded your cover video, it automatically loops without sound and plays when anyone visits your business page. Visitors can turn on the sound by hovering over the video and clicking on it.

Profile Avatars

Your **profile picture** is the small icon that sits on the left of your cover photo. Whenever you write a comment, reply to a comment, or post on your timeline, a small copy of your profile picture will automatically show up.

This image is 170x170 pixels. You can upload a profile picture, by hovering your mouse over the frame of your profile picture (loaded on another site) and choose the option to "upload photo." Then pick your best image and download it to your business page. Even though you can only use a single image as a profile picture, you can update it whenever you feel necessary. You may want to establish a separate photo library where you can store extra cover and profile photos and change them whenever you want to.

I have always found it best to use a picture that is square-shaped; however, Facebook does give you the chance to crop your profile image out of whatever photo you decide to use. Although your profile picture is far smaller than your cover photo, it is still important to use a high-quality, professional photo that represents your business in the best light.

While most businesses choose to use a good picture of their company logo as their profile picture, some businesses will use a photo of a key product. A personal photo is rare, but it's useful if your business offers a service where you are the representative the customers will work with. If you run a personal tutoring service, you can defuse potential unease by providing a headshot to show your target audience who will be doing the tutoring.

Timeline Imagery

When it comes to displaying **images on your timeline**, there are several options available to you. Each single photo you upload onto your timeline will be compressed by Facebook to 476x714 pixels. This image will appear in preview mode; then, when someone clicks on the picture, they will then get to see the entire image.

If you choose to upload a group of several photos together, they will be displayed in the dimensions of the largest image. Vertical and horizontal photos will usually be loaded together. Since this is dependent on the shape and size, you may find that one will become the main image and be displayed as a larger snapshot than the rest.

If you want, you can let other users post their photos on your timeline. However, you do have the ability to prevent others from posting pictures on your page. To accomplish either permission to post or disallowing other users' photos, select settings, and set the box that enables the function.

Posting Links

If you choose to share a link via your timeline, simply paste the URL into the text box along with your personal message. A 476x249 pixel image related to the linked page will be displayed in a preview format. The name of the page connected to the link will also be shown under the preview picture with a brief description of the page. Once this thumbnail image and description appears, you can delete the URL you pasted.

Using Videos

Video is the most rapidly expanding area of Facebook. This medium provides the perfect showcase for any type of business. Statistics show that videos hold the attention longer than static images, so if you have a choice, use a video instead of a still shot.

It is as easy to upload videos to your business pages as still images. It is possible to load your videos onto outside video hosting sites – such as YouTube – and then link to them, but your business will not reap the benefits of engagement that are available when you upload directly to Facebook, so why would you bother to do that? If you've grabbed your audience's attention in a Facebook video, it's a simple matter to direct viewer traffic toward your website for more in-depth information, to engage with you directly, or better yet, to provide an opportunity to make a purchase.

You'll want to center your video on a topic that is trending and try to engage with the minds of your audience. At the end of your video, invite interaction by encouraging the viewer to like or share it.

A recent Nielson study reported that most of our recall of advertising occurs within the first ten seconds. Therefore, instead of uploading an exhaustive video, you would be better served to use a short video clip to capture the imagination of your audience and then invite them to learn more by clicking a link to your website.

Now for the technical details. When recording videos to post on Facebook, the optimum resolution size is 720p. Even though you can upload videos in any digital format, the best are .mov or.mp4, since these formats prefer quality over compression.

While it is important for your video to have superior sound quality, it is even more essential for your video to be interesting without sound. A running transcription allows people to get your message, even if they don't have the ability to hear the audio portion of your recording.

You'll want to capture and focus viewers' attention immediately, during the first few seconds of play. Keep in mind that your videos will be running without sound until the user clicks on the image to activate the audio. It's important to start the video with something that will pique curiosity or entice the viewer to want to watch more.

For the same reason you will need to carefully select the thumbnail image that represents your video. You can choose this by hovering your mouse over your video and choosing the appropriate options on the pop-up menu.

Go Live

Facebook Live enables users to live stream video to their audience, essentially bringing them into the moment with you. Research has revealed that people are three times more likely to watch a live streaming video than something pre-recorded. Businesses can utilize live streaming to include an audience in the broadcast of their special events, product launches, and slice-of-life postings.

Extended Length Videos

Apart from Facebook live, you also have the option to upload prerecorded videos that are more than 20 minutes long, or mini-movies. Most of the time, you'll want to keep your videos short and concise, three minutes at the most but sometimes the situation may call for a longer presentation. If you're publishing an extended lecture, a webinar, or a long musical performance, however, you'll need a longer video.

Promoting Your Videos

As soon as you have uploaded your video to your business page, it's time to start targeting your audience. Just look for the "Boost

Post" button that will be located under your published video. When you click on the button it will take you to an additional page where you can select where your Facebook business page is shown and then target it toward a specific audience. This feature allows you to target specific countries and states and select how many days the video will appear, for up to two weeks.

Auto-Play

I typically prefer to use the auto-play feature. When you upload your videos directly to your Facebook business page, they will appear on a user's timeline and begin playing automatically. Videos uploaded using a third-party link will not. If most of your business videos are hosted on a different video site, you will still be able to upload them to Facebook, but you will only want to upload the ones that work best with Facebook. In other words, only use videos that are short and relevant. If necessary, you might also consider editing your video, shortening it to a length that is more appropriate for Facebook. You have the option then to add a message to the end of the video directing the viewers to the longer version; this will also mean more traffic through your social media outlets.

When you upload your videos directly to Facebook, you have the option of embedding their links in other locations, such as your blog or website. By doing this, your videos will grab more views and thereby boost interaction on your business page. Embedding a Facebook video in your blog or website is easy to do; just click the arrow you see in the upper right corner of your video and choose "embed." This will generate a box with a code. You then need to paste this code to your website or blog and publish it. This video will then appear automatically whenever anyone views your blog or website.

The Playlist

After you have uploaded a suitable number of videos to your business page, you will want to organize them into a playlist. This makes it easy for your audience to identify the videos they intend to view.

Creating a playlist is a straightforward process. Simply go to the video manager and use the option to create a playlist. When you have chosen this option, a box will pop up and you can create a unique name for the playlist and a brief description. Click "next" and Facebook will open a window that allows you to select videos for inclusion in your playlist. Click next and your playlist is ready for use.

Diversify Your Content

People like Facebook business pages because they can stay informed easily. Rather than posting the same type of content each day, your business page will be more interesting to your audience if change things up. Post something completely different to keep the attention of your followers. Remember, people take in information in diverse ways. Some people prefer to read the information while others are more visual and would rather learn things by watching a video. I have found that mixing text posts with other content, such as videos and still images, has proven the best way to engage with my audience. I also throw in a trivia quiz every now and then to tempt my audience to interact, not only with me but also with each other as well.

Ask Questions

If you do it right, asking questions of your audience can open a firestorm of participation. In addition to boosting audience loyalty, you can use questions to gather information for demographic research. Or, you can issue your query just for the fun of it.

If you decide to ask a question to stimulate audience participation, you'll want to word it so that the answer can be kept to a single word or phrase. Anything longer takes the fun out of the game.

People love to talk about themselves, so you will see the most interaction if you ask your audience to share their opinion or state their preference. You can even ask your audience to help make a minor business decision, like choosing the name of an upcoming product.

Use your audience's responses as an opportunity to interact with people outside of your product-related business. This will humanize your business, making it more attractive to your potential customers. People always prefer doing business with a friend than with a stranger; anything you can do to build a person-to-person connection with your audience will always be to your advantage.

Post Boldly

Do not hesitate to post content that other businesses avoid. By this I *don't* mean anything offensive or obnoxious, just something that is totally different from the norm. You want to provoke thought and responses without offending, if possible. You will generally receive a huge positive response to this content, because people like to be surprised by something unique.

Even if a post is met with negative responses, learn from them, apologize to those who are offended, and move on to something else. There's nothing wrong with shaping your content according to what is trending. It makes sense to choose topics that people already have on their minds. But you'll want to try to find a unique angle; don't just parrot what others are saying, but boldly stick out your neck and say what you truly think. You usually won't get your head chopped off, but even if you do, you will have stimulated a response and encouraged interaction with and between your followers. Most people have strong opinions when it comes to trending topics and they are more likely to share their opinions and get involved if you give them an opportunity to discuss the topic further.

Plan Your Posts

Personally, I have found the most effective strategy for posting a good mix of content involves using a calendar to plan out my posts ahead of time. That way, I can ensure a healthy variety in my postings. I can balance more intense topics with lighter content and sprinkle in a good dose of humor to even out the mix.

The calendar allows you to also take full advantage of what is trending to engage with your audience around seasonal topics. Posting content relevant to Christmas at the beginning of December is one example. You can tie the needs of the season to your products, with special offers to celebrate appropriate holidays and national days and sales to punctuate tax season or other days that have special significance.

Optimize Your Posting Times

By researching when most of your target audience is active on Facebook, you can choose the most strategic times to post your varied content, thus maximizing engagement with the various sectors of your audience. Facebook's news feed algorithm ranks what the users see based on their previous interactions with your business page, the type of content it includes, and the newness of your post. If an audience member has interacted consistently with your Facebook page and the page is updated to include a video, there is a high probability that your audience member will see the post when the view is refreshed.

Many recent studies suggest that posting at the end of a week when people may not be at work is ideal. It is, of course, your choice, but I would disagree; you ideally want your posts to appear when people are online to catch them when they're fresh. Whenever you decide to post, you'll want to stay online for a while afterward to be able to respond to comments fairly quickly and thus encourage user interaction.

The easiest way to develop your own posting schedule would be to determine – from your insights page – when your posts are being viewed, and then to post during that window. MarketingCharts.com has reported that Facebook posts reach the first 50 percent of their audience within 30 minutes of the time they are published. Thus, you will reach the bulk of your audience, if they are online, within half an hour of your posting.

It is just as important to consider the lifestyle of your audience, as this can help you schedule your posts. If your targeted audience consists primarily of college students who will be in class during the day, your posts will be most likely to catch them when they're active on Facebook in the evening. By comparison, their teachers will tend to be active online in the morning, since they're busy grading papers in the evening.

Certain kinds of posts have specific times of day when they are best received. When I was a student, I always read the news first thing in the morning. I would welcome informative posts early in the day but would be glad to find a fun video in the evening as I was winding down and relaxing

Let yourself be guided by the times that your audience comments on your page. If you can find a time when your competition is inactive on Facebook, but your audience is online, take advantage of the opening to post at that time.

Look Around

If you are ever short on ideas or you find that your content is not getting the results you had expected, check the pages of your competitors or similar businesses and look at the way that they strategize their content. I am not suggesting that you copy what they are doing; however, there is nothing wrong with getting some ideas about what your audience is looking for. This can be time-consuming but can also result in some important and valuable information.

Look at the subjects that other businesses are posting and note the time of day they favor. Read a specific post, noting the people who have made comments. Although some individuals may be totally private, chances are you will come across a few whose names are public. You can research information about these readers, learning about their interests and noting the similarities. This will give you a better feel for what content will be best received.

Audience Building

Probably the main aim for Facebook business page owners is to find, create and keep building and maintaining their target audience. Social authority is something obtained only by pages with millions of likes, but this does not stop any business from reaching for this goal. The businesses that have social authority and recognition are those national brands and businesses with household names that have been trading for years. The mistake that many smaller businesses make is thinking that the more likes they attract, the more engagement they will have and those likes will turn into purchases. Lots of likes can boost your page's social standing, but unfortunately, many likes do not always translate into dollars earned.

There is no doubt that quality will win over quantity every time. You may only have ten active members in your audience but as long as they are the right people, your audience will grow. For example, suppose you invent a new kind of trainer but you cannot get people interested because they know very little about you. However, if you invite Mo Farah to wear your shoes and he is suitably impressed, the chances are that he will start to promote your shoes to his fans and they will then want to try these shoes. Therefore, if your business page starts with just a handful of people who are interested in your business, make sure you post valuable content. If your content is worth sharing, over time your audience will grow into a group of hardcore fans.

Audience building requires more than high quality, fully optimized content. While your page will generate followers, you should consider taking the following steps to make sure that your page has the maximum exposure, so you can efficiently build your audience further.

Freebies

There are some readers who will like your page for personal reasons. As this could be watching out for updates, it is always best practice to give these readers a reason to follow you and your page. The most beneficial way of doing this is to give the follower something in return for them liking your page. It has become common practice for business pages to offer discount vouchers, additional content and so on in return for readers liking their page.

This is the perfect opportunity to be honest and explain to your followers exactly what they will get and how it will be beneficial to them to like your page. Another viable strategy that you can combine with this is to encourage these followers to invite their friends to like your page. You may decide to offer a discount voucher for a coffee for liking your page and an additional free chocolate bar if they get ten of their friends to like your page.

Many business owners do not know that they can tag their followers in status updates. If your customer, Emma Long, is your 50th follower, you could post, "Big thank you to Emma Long for being our 50th like!" as a status update. To tag one of your followers, you'll simply add an "@" before their name. Tagging is another way to connect with your audience on a personal level; it allows you to create a truly personal experience.

Hashtags

One of the greatest marketing tools established in recent years is the hashtag. Hashtags began gaining popularity on the social media site Twitter, then approximately three years ago they were introduced on Facebook. A hashtag is a phrase or word that has the "#" written in front of it. For example, if you were reading a cookbook by Weight Watchers, you could post your opinion and follow this up with #Weight Watchers.

When you upload any post that includes a hashtag, you can see everybody who has used the same hashtag, and this also becomes clickable. You can make your page more appealing to your target audience by including a hashtag in the hopes that they will find your posts when they are doing an interest search and will go on to like your page. Hashtags should be used carefully and only when they are relevant. Keep your hashtags short and create your own when it makes sense for your business.

Linking to Your Page

Add a clickable button on your business website that can take visitors immediately to your Facebook business page. The best place to add this link is on the homepage or the most viewed part of your website. If you already receive a high volume of website traffic, you can divert this to your Facebook page, as well.

You can also include a link on any other form of social media you use. The simplest way to provide a powerful signature is to display your name prominently, including your title and your social media links. Instead of pasting a link to your page, try using anchor text that states, "Facebook" and then insert a hyperlink to your page.

Coupling this with a request addressed to your target audience usually works incredibly well. If you're the owner of a café, a bulletin that reads, "Want a free coffee? If so, like our Facebook page!" would draw a considerable audience.

Adding Advertising

If your business already has plenty of customers, advertising your Facebook business page will undoubtedly increase your likes significantly. If your business operates purely online, you only need to send your customers an announcement or a newsletter that includes information about your Facebook business page.

If you are running a physical business, you have a lot more flexibility. When I shop locally, I cannot help but notice that the number of businesses attracting high foot traffic also display signs to encourage shoppers to like their Facebook business pages. Customers can be encouraged to like your page by advertising on things your customers will see. I've seen invitations on sales bags, business cards, even on front doors.

Guest Blogging

Another powerful tool from a marketing perspective is guest-blogging. Guest-blogging can be described as writing a blog or an article with the sole purpose of posting on another person's business site, sharing your knowledge and expertise on a subject they know little about. Other business owners are particularly open to guest-blogging, as it is a free way to get content. From your point of view, it is a way to network, expose your business to potential new customers, and – most importantly – share a link to your own Facebook business page. Inviting other business owners to guest blog on your business page benefits you as well and builds goodwill within the marketplace.

Once you start looking, you'll find plenty of places to link to your Facebook business page to get additional instant promotion. If your business accesses other social media sites, you can easily add a link to your page. Twitter and YouTube offer an "about" tab where you can give users linkage to your Facebook page. If you are interacting on a forum where you can discuss your expertise, add a link to your page. If you are established as an expert in a specific field, take the time to answer visitors' questions; this will boost your reputation and build visibility that will translate back to brand awareness.

The possibilities for promoting your business Facebook page are endless. Now it is your chance to take advantage of and apply all of these new things you have learned!

Chapter 6: Creating Incredible Facebook Ads, Events, and Competitions

When you look at the marketing possibilities for your Facebook business page, you will soon understand that this goes farther than simply optimizing your page and making sure you have high quality content. For this reason, this chapter will be dedicated to the marketing aspects which can enhance your Facebook business page, and which are often misunderstood or not taken advantage of.

Ads

Facebook offers paid advertisements that they then promote using the mechanics in the same way as television advertising. It is not hard to create an advertisement for your business; just follow the points below to get started:

Access your "**Ad Manager**" by typing "Ad Manager" In the search field.

When the Ad Manager opens you will find by default that you have accessed your campaigns screen. From here you can view details of your existing campaigns, complete with a full analysis of how they have performed.

Click "**Create campaign.**"

You are now prompted to choose your **objective** from three categories:

- Realization

- Deliberation

- Modification

Each of these categories contains a minimum of one goal to choose, such as:

Realization

- Awareness of your brand, by reaching a wider audience of potential customers

- Having your advertisement seen by the highest number of users possible

Deliberation

- Sending more people to your website or third-party location

- Engaging and interacting with your target audience to gain more likes

- Increasing the volume of people choosing to install and use your apps

- Offering the choice for more people to view your videos

- Increasing your sales through potential customers

Modification

- Converting new customers from your potential target audience

- Providing your target audience with a catalogue to promote sales

- Promoting and driving more people to visit your store

Targeting

Facebook offers a powerful feature in the form of marketing, which allows businesses and individuals to create advertisements targeted to people through their interests. This feature is known as **"detailed targeting."** When a business creates an advertisement with the sole aim of covering specific interests, Facebook will then target the people who share these interests with that ad.

Previously Facebook allowed only one target interest per campaign; for example, if you were a design agency creating specialist website designs for Apple users, the logical audience would consist of all people who owned or liked Apple products. However, Facebook would only allow you to target either those who owned the product or those who liked and aspired to own the product.

This may not sound like a big deal, if there were 50,000 people who owned Apple products and 50,000 people aspiring to own the product, your target audience would be 100,000, but as it was your advertisement would only be seen by half of your potential audience. Fortunately, Facebook has changed the way this operates, allowing businesses to target many interests per ad. It also gives the business the choice to exclude interests from their advertisement if they deem this necessary.

When you are using the Ad Manager tool to set up your advertisement, there is a section labeled "**Interests**". As you type a term you wish to use for targeting, such as "Apple products," a drop-down menu will appear that offers specific matches via Facebook. Therefore, using the same example as above, by typing in "Apple owners", Facebook will present you with the official Facebook page for Apple and you have instant access to this audience. You can narrow the options further. For example, if you typed "iPad" you would have access and be connected to those people who liked Apple products and those who liked the iPad.

Events on Facebook

An excellent way to address your target audience to an announcement or provide information regarding an up-and-coming promotion is to use Facebook events.

When you create an event for your business page, you follow the same procedure as you would when creating an event from your personal Facebook account. However, you cannot send direct invitations to your business followers. You are also not allowed to send emails to the people who are attending. You can get around this by posting the event on your personal timeline, join the event from your timeline and then invite your friends. Once the event is posted those fans of your page would be able to invite their friends too.

How to create an Event

1. Start by clicking the **"Offer"** and **"Event"** buttons on your timeline.

2. Add all the details for the event such as date, location, etc. Just remember that if you are using any images they must be a minimum of 714 x 264 pixels

3. Finally, add the link which takes people to the place where tickets can be redeemed. This link could be to your own external website.

When you are creating a business event, from personal experience I would advise that you have a page to announce the event other than on Facebook. This could be an event website or your business website.

At this time, Facebook cannot support the sale of tickets, but among the most popular sales integration are Eventpal and Eventbrite. When your event is finalized, this can be shared with your followers by activating the share button, and don't forget to pin the event to the top of your business page.

Event Promotion

To make sure that you get maximum exposure for your event, the following strategies should be followed to obtain complete promotion:

Event buzz

Prior to creating your event on Facebook, you ideally want to create buzz to get your audience excited. To get things started, you can make a teaser announcement that you are having an event and that people should keep checking back for more details.

- Cover Photo

  Your cover photo is an excellent way to grab the attention of new visitors and to promote your event. From here you can either encourage new visitors to click on your cover photo, which will take them to an external link, or have an arrow that points at your events tab under your cover photo. This is a powerful way to promote your event as well as to grab the attention of new visitors to your page. When you change or add a new cover photo this will show in your **News Feed** for your audience to see.

- Facebook Advertising to Promote Your Event

  Once you have created your event, you will be offered the chance to promote it immediately. Simply click **"Promote"** and you will see the **Event Responses** page. From here you can set your budget and the audience that you want to target.

- Post Promotion

  An effective way to promote your post to your target audience and their friends is to target people who have no connection to your page. Use your event photo, click **"Boost Post"** and this will then pin the event to the top of your page. Remember to add the call-to-action, asking users to share your event.

- Event Reposting

  In the weeks leading up to your event, you should repost the details about your event, varying the time of day, to help ensure that your audience knows about your event. You'll want to post additional event details, as this will keep the interest going and create the buzz.

- Everyone Loves an Offer

  There is no doubt that everybody loves an offer, and this is a fantastic way to provide your audience with something that is beneficial to them.

- Friend invites

  While you are unable to invite your followers to an event from your business page, this can be overcome by joining the event through your personal page timeline, as this will then give you the opportunity to invite your friends. When friends then respond to the event, they can invite their friends using the tab on the event page.

- Make Everywhere Your Target.

  Make sure that you announce the details of your event on every possible medium, such as your blog, articles, social media sites, website and so on.

- Email

  Not all of your customers are going to be fans of your Facebook page; so, you'll want to also utilize email and other media options to notify your audience of your planned event.

Competition benefits

Many of the businesses owners I have spoken to reported seeing enormous success from running a competition on a Facebook business page. A Facebook competition is a brilliant way to generate engagement and garner new leads for your business. Over recent years, Facebook has become more relaxed with the rules; now it allows businesses to run competitions from their own pages. This has made the entire process easier and cheaper, an advantage for the smaller business owner. You still need to check the terms and conditions, as Facebook does not allow liking a page or sharing a post to serve as a competition entry or as a condition to entry.

Before you create your competition, you should be clear about what you want to achieve from your competition. There are many benefits to be achieved by running a competition from your business Facebook page including:

- Building an audience

    A competition can quickly boost your number of followers and increase the likes for your business page. You need to be aware that Facebook does not allow liking as a condition for entering the competition. Sweepstake style competitions are the most popular type of competition to increase likes for your business page.

- Increasing Engagement

    One guaranteed way to increase the engagement and your business' EdgeRank score is to invite your audience to share your competition. EdgeRank is an algorithm used by Facebook, which chooses the stories that show on the user's news feed. The algorithm scores each story and then displays only those that have scored well. One way to create a lot of interest in your business page is to run a photography competition as this will encourage fans to comment on the photos and begin sharing them with each other.

- Email capturing

  When you run a competition, competitors will join your audience by opting in. This is excellent as you will then be half-way to converting your competitors' likes into your customers.

- Building brand awareness and social proof

  Having large numbers of people liking your page helps to build your social proof, and any promotion like this will help to increase awareness of your brand and business.

- Rewarding your audience

  When you give your followers the chance to win something that they value, this helps to keep their interest, particularly if you offer everybody a money-off coupon as a reward for entering.

- Increasing traffic to your site

  A competition can drive considerable traffic to your business site by asking your audience to find certain information about the products shown on your website, then to complete their entry form.

How to Create Your Competition

There are two ways that you can create a competition: either directly on your own page or by using a third-party app.

Running your own competition directly on your timeline, is cheap and straightforward. Competitions can create a lot of interest on your page, particularly if you are asking for some type of action to be taken.

Here are some ideas for creating competitions on your timeline:

- Comments Competition

  You post a picture and ask your fans to comment on it. This is an effective way of creating a buzz around a new product that you may be about to launch.

- Likes Competition

  This type of competition is incredibly easy to enter. Participants enter the competition by liking a post.

- Caption Competition

  This type of competition is great fun and gives your fans a chance to get creative. You only need to upload a compelling image and ask your fans to write a caption. The most original caption wins.

- Fill-In-The-Blanks Competition

  Another fun idea is to pick a subject that relates to your brand, write a sentence, and leave a space blank for your fans to complete.

- Photography Competition

  Photography competitions are popular. You can either ask your fans to submit their pictures by attaching them to a private message or ask them to post them on your wall.

- Question and Answers Competition

  This is an effective way of getting your audience to find out about one of your products. Simply ask your audience a question about a product of yours and let the communication flow from this point onward.

- Ideas Competition

71

Get your fans to participate by asking for their ideas to resolve a problem. It could be that you are looking for a name for a new product. This type of competition shows that you value the opinions of your fans and it can make them feel a part of your brand.

How to Run A Successful Competition

To get the best results, I offer a few tips for running competitions on your Facebook timeline:

- Post a good image – Using a good image with a description helps to tempt your fans into entering and sharing your competition.

- Make your cover photo the competition image – Make sure that you direct people to where they can enter to win.

- Have a clear headline and call-to-action – Make it clear in the first sentence what you want your fans to do.

- Provide a clear description –Make it easy for your fans to understand how to enter and what they can win.

- Establish a page to collect entries – If your aim is to collect email addresses, you need to create a page either on your website or on a separate landing page.

- Select the ideal prize – The type of prize you intend to offer is important and it should relate to your line of business. By doing this, your competition is far more likely to appeal to your targeted audience and attract fans who are sincerely interested in what you have to offer.

- Determine the length of the competition – You need to decide how long your competition is going to run. Video and photography competitions need a longer run than say a sweepstake, which can be much shorter.

- Post rules that are simple and clear –You can include the rules in the post or create an external web page for the rules of the competition. Your rules should:

    o Establish how many times a fan can enter

    o Post the deadline for the winner to claim their prize

    o Provide the closing date

    o Determine who is eligible

    o Inform how winners are selected

    o Include the term **"Void where Prohibited"** – by doing this you will stay in compliance with any country or state regulations banning your competition.

- Announce the winner – For competition results you can announce the winner on your timeline. This ensures that entrants must return to your page to find out who the winner is.

Creating A Competition Through A Third-Party App

If you want to launch your competition without the hassle or worry of administering it, using a third-party app is ideal. Apps have lots of advantages, particularly if you want to attract many entrants and want to collect emails and add sharing functionality. For larger audiences and sweepstakes, using a third-party app looks professional and it is far easier for you to collect emails and add functionality for sharing your competition.

Third party applications:

- Look professional

73

Third party apps can make your competition look organized and professional, both of which will help to create the trust of your entrants.

- Provide Email capture

  Using a third-party app means that you can collect email addresses when your users enter your competition.

- Share functionality

  Third-party apps usually include a feature where entrants are offered the opportunity to share the competition.

- Manage winner selection

  Using a third party takes care of all the administration involved when it comes to selecting and notifying the winner.

- Provide "thank you" coupons

  It is easy to create a thank you coupon for all the entrants so that everyone who enters is rewarded; this is also an effective way to drive sales conversions.

Third party apps also help to get more likes, more conversions, more shares, greater engagement, and more emails.

Promoting your competition

Regardless of whether you decide to create your competition on your timeline or use a third-party app, you still need to gain as much exposure as possible.

Here are some ideas for promoting an upcoming competition

- Create a buzz prior to the competition launch – To create some excitement before the competition is announced, you can offer a teaser and ask your fans to watch out for the new competition. You could also ask your fans what prize they would value the most.

- Promotional post – Upload your image with text about the competition and a link to the landing page.

- Create a Facebook ad – This is a way of widening your audience enormously. Just click on the Advertisements Manager from your page and then Create Ad.

- Repost your competition – Reposting your competition at various times running up to the competition expiry date will let as many people as possible see the competition in their News Feed.

- Announce the competition on other social platforms – You can use hashtags on Facebook and Twitter so people who are looking for competitions will find you. Use keywords such as competitions, win, photo competition, sweepstakes and so on.

- Pin to top – Pin your competition image up on the top of your page so that visitors will see it first.

- Change cover photo – Adding your competition image to your cover photo ensures that any new visitor to your page will see the competition, and it will also appear in the News Feed of your fans.

- Encourage others to share your competition – Adding a call-to-action is a wonderful way to prompt people to spread the word.

- Promote your competition on your website – Make sure that you have a banner for your competition on your website.

- Email – You may have customers who are not fans on Facebook; Emailing all your contacts will inform them and give everyone the opportunity to enter your competition.

- Google Adwords – You can use Google Adwords to drive traffic to either Facebook or a separate competition landing page.

- Competition sites – There are many websites where competition details can be added.

- Offline promotion – Make sure to add the details of your competition to any marketing materials, receipts, bills and so on.

Analyzing the results

Most third-party applications let you analyze the results by providing you with the appropriate information; they can also compare the effectiveness of your competition with Twitter. You'll be able to see the ways your competition has affected your interaction on Facebook by viewing the insights and comparing your figures from before with the numbers following the competition. It is important here to track how many fans, competitors, likes, and shares you have gained as a result of the competition. You'll also want to note how sales of your products and website visits have been impacted.

Tracking all this information will enable you to create new competitions and improve the results in the future. Measuring results lets you know whether your competition has worked or not. From the results, you may decide that you need to promote more on weekends or a certain time of the day.

Chapter 7: Creating World Class Content

Now that you have your business page up and running on Facebook and you are starting to gain "likes" and building an audience, you're on your way. However, keep in mind that once users have chosen to like your page, the chances are they will never return to your page again. Statistics show that 90 percent of fans never return.

To create your own community of followers who will subscribe to your newsletter, share your content and ultimately buy your products or service, you must build trust and likeability. The only way for your business to achieve this is by communicating with your followers regularly and always providing quality content that is not only attention grabbing, but also appeals to their interest and will add some value to their lives. Once your followers start interacting with your content, the trust building can begin with a view to converting these people from followers to customers.

Even when a business starts posting on Facebook, it is unlikely that their posts are going to be seen by every fan in their News Feed unless the business is paying for promoted posts. This is because Facebook uses the EdgeRank algorithm, which determines what does and doesn't show up in a user's timeline. Facebook knows that because of the sheer volume of content that is posted, if their users were exposed to every post it would be overwhelming. For this reason, Facebook developed EdgeRank to provide the best possible experience for every user. EdgeRank helps to ensure that users see what is deemed most important to them and what will give them the most value.

There are three variables that are measured to make up this algorithm:

- Affinity

- Weight

- Time decay

Affinity

Affinity is a measurement of the similarity between the content of your website and the activities of your readers. The more likes and comments a viewer gives you, the more frequently your posts will show up in their news feed.

Weight

Weight measures the value carried by the various type of content. The way in which users engage with a post also affects the score it receives.

Time Decay

Time decay relates to the age of the post. The older the post, the lower the score will be. This is what helps your News Feed to stay full of fresh, new content. Research shows that approximately 75 percent of engagement takes place within the first four hours and the value of the post decreases as time moves on.

One of the main goals for creating content for Facebook as a business is to produce the highest quality content for your audience so that they will engage with your content, thereby creating the highest possible EdgeRank score. The higher the score, the more fans will see and engage with your posts. Businesses can check their EdgeRank score using this link: www.edgerankchecker.com

To create just the right content, you need a real understanding of your target audience and a deep insight into what interests and motivates them. Armed with this information, along with additional tactics outlined in this book, you will be well prepared to develop your very own community of followers who believe in what you have to offer and, more importantly, will tell everyone they know.

It's time to look at the various kinds of posts and find some helpful tips to help you create the best experience for your fans. These are the things that can boost your engagement levels and give you the highest EdgeRank.

Content Ideas

With all the competition on the internet vying for attention, the only way your business is going to win is by having high quality content. There is no doubt that content is king on Facebook. This is even more important now that Facebook is decreasing the number of posts from pages which are visible in the News Feed.

It can be a challenge to produce compelling content for your audience time after time, on into the foreseeable future. When you have chosen your topic of content, you may be pleasantly surprised at how often this idea leads to several others, meaning that you can create many pieces of quality content.

Here are some ideas for content that can be adapted to any type of business or topic:

1. **Related Information and Content**

    The most shared type of content on Facebook is relatable. This means that your content should include anything that your target audience can relate to and identify with. It is when your audience sees a piece of content and immediately thinks, "I can relate to that and this is exactly how I feel when this happens. I know just what she means." It is incredibly powerful because this content is immediately communicating to your audience that you understand them and feel their joy or pain and can empathize with them. With relatable content you are communicating with your fans on a deep level, which all helps to build trust and relationships.

2. **Emotive Content**

79

Evoking an emotional response is an essential ingredient to successful viral content marketing. If you create content that evokes a strong positive emotional response, it will help your audience associate that emotion with your brand. Content like this is very memorable and you can make people feel something by posting an image, text, or video which can help to build your brand and create powerful associations. Evoking any of the primary emotions, whether joy, fear, anger, sadness or even disgust, will compel your readers to respond to your content by commenting and sharing with their friends.

3. Educational Content

Posting informative and educational content about your subject is invaluable. This will make you stand out and be regarded as a leader and expert in your field. Providing valuable and useful content will encourage your followers to return, increasing the chances that they will share your content with their friends. Remember, your audience is looking to find and share valuable content with their friends and customers too and will also want to be associated with any compelling content you create.

4. Informative Content

This could consist of letting your followers know about an upcoming webinar, trade show, or other event in the area. You could also inform your readers of an exclusive offer or anything else that will be of value to them.

5. Amusing/Entertaining Content

The whole point of social media is being social and having fun. People love to share funny stuff. Even if it is not something you have created yourself, if you think it will appeal to your target audience, share it. The aim here is to entertain and amuse your audience. Friends. Humor is an all-round winner, as it not only breaks down barriers, but it is also more likely to be liked and shared.

6. Seasonal Content

Another effective way to stay connected with your audience is to post content related to holidays and annual celebrations. If you have an international audience, go that extra mile and remember their religious celebrations and national holidays; doing so will help you build a more personal connection and relationship with your audience.

7. Motivational/Inspirational Content

Everyone has a difficult day every now and again and will need a little bit of motivation or cheering up. A motivational quote will help to lift your audience and can help you to connect with them. When you understand your audience's desires, what they aspire to, and what are their frustrations, then you will be more easily able to motivate them by posting inspiring content. These posts are also very shareable, especially if put together with a colorful and inspiring photo or cartoon.

8. Employee and Behind-The-Scenes Content

If you have news about your employees and the wonderful things they are doing, post it! Maybe they have been involved in a fundraiser or won an award. Giving your audience a behind-the-scenes view of your business helps to keep your brand and business looking real and authentic and adds a human interest._It's also a morale booster for your employees.

9. Customer Content

Having a member of the month or including news or content about a customer's business is an effective way to spark interest in your posts. Sharing a customer's content not only shows you value your audience but that you can also encourage them to do the same. If you are a B2B, you could invite your audience to network and let them share their page on your page once a month or once a week. This is a terrific way to offer them value. It also creates loyalty, keeps your page in their mind and keeps them coming back to visit your page again and again.

10. Shared Content

While it is great to post most of your own content, do not be afraid to share another person's content as long as it is relevant. Sharing informative content will make you far more valuable to your followers and they will keep returning. Sharing content is also incredibly important in building relationships with your fans. People will be much more open to your brand when you show support for theirs.

11. Statistics

Mark Twain said that there are three kinds of lies: lies, damned lies, and statistics. You'll want to be sure that your statistics aren't any of these three, because people love statistics which relate to your niche. If your business is B2B (Business to Business: a situation where one business makes a commercial transaction with another.), posting statistics can gain a lot of interest, especially if they are displayed in a visually appealing way, perhaps with an infographic or graph. These are more likely to be shared if they can be translated into a useful tip for your audience.

12. Questions

Asking questions about subjects your audience may be interested in is an excellent way to encourage comments, community, and interaction. People love sharing their opinions and thoughts and love the opportunity to communicate, contribute, and be heard. Even if you are just posting a picture or video, make it your practice to ask a question.

13. Top Tens

People love lists about who or what is top or best. Lists spark interest and this is probably because people like comparing their choices and judgments with those of others. Some people want to feel affirmed in their decisions. They want to know that other people are making the same choices, so their opinion must be right. Others are comforted by knowing that their choices are different from the crowd and that they are unique.

14. Controversial Content

Posting a controversial statement is a terrific way to spark a conversation and interaction. People love to voice their opinions, have input and be heard. It is best for your business to stay out of the discussion because you do not want to lose followers and you must be sensitive to your audience so that you do not upset them; therefore, you need to be careful what topics you pick.

15. Special Offers

Social media is a fantastic way to get the message out about any special offers you have running, but you need to be careful not to post them too often or they will end up like advertising and make a "bad noise" in your audience's News Feed. It is important that what you are offering is of real value, exclusive to your fans and that you are offering a deadline by which they must redeem the offer or miss out.

16. Voting Polls and Customer Feedback

Creating a poll is another way to encourage engagement on social media. Using a poll can give you a far greater perspective and understanding of your followers; this in turn will mean that you can collate their important feedback to provide a better service or make changes to your products. You can either ask your audience a question and ask them to like or comment or use an app such as "Poll."

17. Tips and Tricks

Offering a daily or weekly "Top Tip" can keep your audience hooked and returning again and again for the latest information and is a good way to increase loyalty and build relationships. Tips can include anything from step-by-step instructions to information regarding a useful application.

18. News/Current Events

Offering news about the latest developments in your area or industry is a certain way to keep people interested and sharing your content. Being current and up-to-date with local news is useful to your audience and it keeps your business looking fresh. To stay up-to-date, subscribe to News Feeds and blogs that offer news about your industry or local area.

19. Negative content

People like to hear what not to do. For example, ten things not to say at a job interview or things not to do on your first date. The lists of possibilities for this type of post are endless and can create some real amusement and interest.

20. Q & A live session

There is the capacity for you to have your own Q & A session on your Facebook business page. This allows you to create conversation and stimulate engagement. At the same time, it sets forth a professional, informative, and caring image. To set this up, you'll want to establish a specified time of day when fans can post their questions in the comment section of your Facebook post and expect a quick reply. Alternatively, you could ask them to post their questions and give them a day when you will be answering them.

21. Complete the sentence

One way to get your target followers engaged is to engage them in developing content. Fill-in-the-blanks posts are a bit of fun while also creating conversation.

22. Case Studies

Case studies are the best way to demonstrate how something works through real examples. Case studies can show how your customers have used your products or services to benefit them in some way. They can serve to demonstrate a principal or method of doing something, using other businesses as examples.

23. Voting Likes or Shares

This is another fantastic way to get your target market involved with your content. Simply add two images in one post and ask the audience to vote for which image they would choose, either by "liking" or "sharing." This is a quick way to extend your reach and increase your brand's visibility. For this to be successful you need to have a good subject and one that most people can identify with.

24. Blog

Creating regular blog posts is an effective way to get fans onto your blog. Make sure you always include an image to provoke interest. Asking a question can create curiosity and intrigue.

25. Greetings

One way to create positive connections between you and your target audience is to post an attractive image or wish your fans good morning, good night or to enjoy their weekend. This goes a long way to break the ice and build relationships.

26. Reviews & Testimonials

If you have received a good review on Foursquare or Google Places or just a positive message from someone, post it. Posting good things people write or say about you contributes to your social proof and builds trust. Remember, people will believe more what others say about your business than what you, as the owner, say about it.

27. Share something personal

People like to connect with the person behind the brand. If you have your own personal brand, this is important. Sharing interesting and positive snippets about your personal life can help to build relationships and give an authentic feel to your brand. Sharing your plans for the day or posting the occasional photo of yourself can help your audience to know you.

28. Thank your fans

Thanking your fans for their engagement and support shows you truly value and appreciate them. This personal touch is not only courteous, but your gratitude communicates directly to your fans and encourages them to continue participating and engaging with your content in the future.

29. Help your followers

Keeping the lines of communication open by asking your fans what sort of content they want more of is another way of showing your fans that you are there to help them.

30. Personal recommendations

Sharing anything of value with your fans, such as a good book or a useful app, is an excellent way to offer value, and it will help to keep your fans feeling positive about your brand.

Choosing Content to Post on Facebook

The following are tips that I have used to ensure that my business posts only valuable and quality content on Facebook:

- Is this relevant to my audience?

  Whenever you are about post anything, question whether it is relevant and if it isn't, don't use it.

- Post frequently

  To create the greatest opportunity for your fans to see your posts, you need to post between two and four times a day. The average lifespan of a post is three hours, with the major amount of engagement taking place in the first hour.

  Some people may only look at their Facebook page once a day. Balancing your content over various times of the day give your content more chances of being seen by different people. Quality will always win over quantity, so if you can't come up with something good to share, don't publish anything until next time.

- Compelling headlines/introductions

Make sure you always communicate why you are sharing and why you think your post will be interesting to your audience. Not only will this grab their attention, but it also helps to personalize your posts and to begin a conversation.

- Call-to-action

It has been proved that posts with a call-to-action have greater engagement than those posts that have nothing. Your target audience will need a little reminder to like, share and comment and these posts will receive far more engagement than those that don't. Giving your target audience a choice is an effective way to engage them. It is down to you to get your fans to do what you want.

- Questions

The reason people choose to use social media sites is because they like to interact with others. A fantastic way to promote interaction is through asking questions. According to recent statistics, asking questions can double readers' engagement, and is an excellent way to start a conversation.

- Hashtags

We have all heard about hashtags (#) and we mentioned this earlier but let's review and talk about this a bit more - what is a hashtag? Hashtags can turn single words, several words or phrases into a link that can be searched on News Feeds. Every hashtag is provided with a unique URL and when visitors click on the link they can then see posts that contain that hashtag.

It is easy to create a hashtag. All you must do is put the hashtag symbol before the word, words or phrases with no space. Hashtags do not work with mobile phones but work on all desktop computers. Avoid using too many hashtags in a single post or you risk losing your audience to the distraction.

When hashtags are used correctly on Facebook, they can be a huge benefit as they increase your range and give you additional opportunities for your page and content to be seen. If you find a hashtag that has a good following and relates to what you are saying, using this will increase your chances of being seen.

- Pin to the Top

You may have some posts that you believe are particularly important and want new users to see as soon as they visit your page. When you "**Pin to Top**" your post is put in the left at the top of your News Feed. This stays in this position for a week and you can always repeat the process if you want your post there again. To pin a post to the top simply hover your cursor around the top right corner of a post, click the pencil symbol, and select the "Pin to Top" option.

This is a handy feature as you can also use it to tempt users to become fans, drive new people to an offer, or post a welcome video, or a recording of a recent webinar. Regardless of what your promotional goal for the week is, use "**Pin to Top**" to promote the goal properly.

- Promoted Posts

There is just one way you can guarantee that your posts will show up in your friends' News Feed and this is by using promoted posts through the "**Boost Post**" feature. When you use this feature, you must choose whether your post is seen by those who have already liked your page, or whether to use it for targeting. There is a cost for using promoted posts. It is determined by how many people see the post.

How frequently you use promoted posts will depend on your budget. To make the most of your budget, you need to try to promote only the posts that are going to create the most engagement. The best way to gauge this is to watch and see how your fans engage with a post prior to promoting it. Entertaining posts are usually the ones that receive the most engagement rather than sales-driven posts. However, if you do have a good offer or action for your audience to take advantage of, a promoted post will guarantee that as many people see it as possible.

- Scheduling Posts

  Facebook allows you to prepare multiple posts for publication and then schedule precisely when you want them to be released to the public. Scheduling a post is simple. Click the symbol of the clock, enter the day, time and year for when you want the post to load and you're done.

- Add emoticons

  Statistics have shown that adding emoticons can increase engagement by more than 30 percent. You should not overuse emoticons, but they can provide a personal touch every once in a while.

Chapter 8: The Best Marketing Strategies for Facebook

Before you can establish a plan to market your business on Facebook, you need to have an idea of what you can gain through it. Planning is essential to the success of any marketing campaign. Consequently, I have created this chapter to provide you with everything you should consider when you are planning your campaign, before you begin uploading any content.

This includes ways to create your business' mission statement, create aims and purpose, and plan tactics and strategies to assist you in achieving what you want. Finally, we will discuss ways to prepare your business, your website, your blog, and your email campaigns to allow you to capture and convert everyone who shows interest.

Work From a Solid Mission Statement

This is a basic strategy for succeeding in any business. If you've already crafted a mission statement, you will be able to use it as we work through this chapter. If not, you'll want to follow the instructions in this section carefully to define your brand and the audience you wish to target. The mission statement needs to communicate your brand message while describing your promise and commitment.

The following steps will help you create your own mission statement for your business:

1. Describe the purpose of your business and what it offers.

2. Describe your core values and how they contribute to your offering a quality service or product.

3. Describe the levels of customer services you strive to achieve.

4. Describe the commitment your business will provide to your customers.

5. Identify your customer base, for example, other businesses, retail assistants, college students etc.

6. Describe the benefits and values your business can provide to its customers.

Once you have your mission statement complete, anyone who either works with or intends to buy from you will know what is expected of them and how you will see that these expectations are met.

Setting Aims and Purposes

The key to your businesses success on Facebook lies within the aims and purposes you have set. Once you have set them you can begin to plan ways in which you can achieve them.

Aims

An aim should be thought of as the direction in which your business is headed, the course you want your business to follow, and what you intend to accomplish through this business. The following aims are vital for running a business successfully:

- Increase revenue streams and sales

- Reduce business running costs

- Improve and refine customer services

Each of these aims directly affects the others.

Measurable Purpose

When you have set your overall aims for your business, you need to start being more specific. To do this I would advise you to create what is known in the marketing industry as SMART objectives. SMART is an acronym that describes the essential characteristics that define a goal. Below is a brief explanation for these terms:

Specific – looking at areas of your business to improve

Measurable – deciding on how much time you will spend on your aims

Attainable – ensuring that your expectations are realistic

Relevant – your aims need to be relevant to the current climate in which your business is operating

Time-Bound – setting realistic time goals, without which things may not get done

Tactics and Strategies

When you have decided on the aims and purpose for your business, it is time to work out how you intend to achieve these on Facebook. It is time to begin thinking about your tactics and strategies. The following are just a few of the strategies you may wish to employ:

- Create a free offer that has instant email collection to redeem.

- Decide that you will post content x times a day.

- Set your budget for posting x promoted posts each month.

- Set yourself a target to run x competitions on Facebook per year.

- Set aside a predetermined time each day to like other pages that are in some way related your business.

To begin with, you'll want to estimate how much time you will need to do something to achieve something else; however, the general idea is the same. As your campaigns begin to run, you will find that you need to make changes to certain things to achieve what you are aiming for. This could include increasing your spending on promoted posts to reach a wider audience or increasing your spending on additional advertising to gain fans. There is only one way that you can learn how to achieve your aims, and this is by continually monitoring your results against those aims and that purpose and making the changes that are necessary.

Posting Calendar on Facebook

Once you have all your strategies decided and in place, you should know how much and what content type that you need to post to achieve your aims. One of the most demanding tasks of your campaign is providing consistent quality content every day and understanding that you may need to post this content up to four times a day. Although this may sound daunting when you first begin, you will soon see that one idea generally leads to many more.

The Facebook calendar is the perfect way to plan your content for the future; this is how you can ensure that you have consistency in your posting. You will see that there are many online tools and applications that can help you with this. I have found Google calendar good to use, as it allows you to use color coding, which is an excellent way to categorize your posts. Otherwise, you can create a simple calendar using an Excel spreadsheet.

You'll want to think through how you'll structure your posts. Some themes may be immediately apparent, so you'll want to plan specific posts around the different main themes. For example, you could choose to post around a selected theme on each Monday. All you need to remember is that you must have a good variety of posts to keep your audience interested. From here you can break the year into months, weeks, etc. and create your personal schedule. To this schedule you can add things you have planned for your business, such as product launches, competitions, offers and so on, and then add special dates such as public holidays. Finally, you need to incorporate all this information into your daily plan.

Having completed this, I realize just how scary it can be to sit in front of a blank calendar but breaking it down will make it far easier for you to collate and bring everything together. By using a calendar, you can keep your campaign in check, focus on your marketing aims and keep things balanced regarding your subjects and type of media you plan to use. The calendar allows you to look to the future, which in turn will assist you to combine your marketing efforts with your Facebook business campaign.

Stand-Out Marketing

Following your aims and purpose will guide you toward a successful campaign, but how can you stand out on Facebook with so many other businesses competing for the attention of millions of readers? If you have found yourself following any of the larger brands on social media, it will soon become apparent that certain brands stand head and shoulders above the rest. In general, these are businesses and brands that seem to be bigger than their products.

You will find that these are the businesses that have the highest quality content, an immense and highly targeted audience and the greatest amount of interaction and engagement. Their audience hangs on everything they say, and they achieve huge volumes when it comes to the open rate for emails that they send.

It is obvious that these businesses and brands understand and can relate to their audience fully and offer everything their audience wants, such as making their dreams come true, offering them exceptional value and otherwise meeting their needs. These businesses have built this respectful, loving audience and it is a fact that this will transfer down and be reflected in their profits.

The best way to understand these "Social Media Superstars" is to think about a person you know who is always the life and soul of a situation, people appear to be drawn to them, surround them and hang onto everything they say while also having a wonderful time. For some reason these types of people also come across as the most interesting and interested, the most charismatic while also being excellent listeners. Now the question is how you can follow this example and what do you need to do to stand out with your Facebook business marketing? These brands and businesses stand out because they have done the research and know about their audience and what it is they are looking for.

Your goal is to create something that will be of benefit to your business, but to make this happen you need to bow to your audience and what they want. At the same time that you are giving your audience what they are looking for by solving their problems or simplifying their lives, you will grow an audience that trusts you, values your wisdom, and eventually makes a purchase from you.

This audience will transfer into ambassadors for your business and work for you by sharing content and promoting your business in the most powerful way, by word-of-mouth. To stand out from the competition you need to go that little bit extra and make sure you complete the goals set out below:

- Commit fully, be positive about your campaign, and understand that you need to play the long game to truly see results.

- Believe in what you offer, whether a product, a service, or your very person.

- Know your audience, what they like and need and how you can communicate with them.

- Put your audience and their needs first at all times.

- Listen to your audience, understand and embrace options to converse with them.

- Offer free advice and information.

- Be true to your brand.

Quick Tip: Remember, it is your audience that is important. Provide them with what they want, and you won't go far wrong.

Chapter 9: How To Be Successful With Facebook Advertising

Facebook has created a hugely effective and user-friendly advertising platform for use by their customers which has been designed initially with businesses in mind to advertise to their target audience. As reaching your audience for free is becoming more difficult, paying for the attention on Facebook is becoming more necessary, especially if you are offering a specific promotion.

Facebook keeps an enormous amount of information on its users, which includes:

- Age

- Gender

- Location

- Interests

Because this information is available, it is easy for businesses to leverage the power of Facebook to reach their target audience. Businesses can target users based upon the groups that they have joined and the pages they have liked. That's right - it is easy for businesses to target the fans of their competition! Targeting advertisements to fans of your own page can help drive down the cost of advertising considerably. Businesses can use Facebook advertising to either advertise their page or to drive traffic to an external blog or website.

Depending upon the advertising objectives of your business, there are a variety of possible advertising options available to you on Facebook. Here are some of the most useful.

Promoted Page Posts

Promoting your posts will help them show up in other people's timelines, as well as their friends'

Quick Tip:

- Page Post requirements:

  Text – 90 characters

  Image size 1200 x 1200 pixels

- Page Post Link Ad:

  Text 90 characters

  Link title 25 characters,

  Image size – 1200 x 627 pixels

Getting More Likes

You can create advertisements to grow your audience on Facebook, and this is incredibly important if you want to succeed on Facebook. Once readers like your page you have a far better chance to build trust and convert them into customers.

Quick Tip:

- Text 90 characters

- Image size 1200 x 450 pixels

More Clicks to Your Website

Facebook enables you to advertise your external blog or website.

Quick Tip:

- Text 90 characters

- Advertisement image size 1200 x 864 pixels

Website Conversions

Facebook lets you create advertisements for actions that you want your audience to take on your external website. You should use a conversion tracking pixel to gauge your results.

Quick Tip:

- Text 90 characters,

- Image size 1200 x 864 pixels

App installations

This offers you the opportunity to create an advertisement which encourages users to install your app.

Quick Tip:

- Text 90 characters

- Image size 1200 x 864 pixels

Increase App Engagement

This gives you the opportunity to create an advertisement that will give you more activity on your app.

Increase Event Attendance

This provides you with the opportunity to create advertisements that will promote your event.

Quick Tip:

- Text 90 characters

- Event title 25 characters

- Image size 1200 x 450 pixels

Create Offers That Are Redeemable in Your Store.

This gives you the opportunity to either create an offer or advertise an offer you have created and placed on your timeline.

Quick Tip:

- Text 90 characters

- Offer title 25 characters

- Image size 1200 x 627pixels

How to create your Facebook Ad

It is simple to create an advertisement to place on your Facebook business page, and Facebook provides an easy to follow guide to make this even easier. It is important that you select and upload an image, create your headline and description, select your audience, and decide on the placement for your ad. The tips below are some I found useful when creating my advertisements:

- **Study other ads** - Pay attention to the advertising that appears on your News Feed and notice especially the ones that attract your attention.

- **Image** - Your image is more important than any other part of your ad, as it is what will grab the attention of your audience. If your aim is to increase your page likes, then Facebook will automatically populate your advertisement with your page's cover photo. If you then choose an advertisement which will appear to the right of your News Feed, a close-up image will show up better. You can find images on Facebook in their library or other stock photo sites. You may also want to consider using an online image editor such as www.picmonkey.com to enhance, add effects and edit your images.

- **Headline** - It is important to use a headline that will grab the reader's attention while staying within the 25-maximum character limit.

- **Text** - An effective advertisement describes the important benefits to your audience, creates desire and ends with a call-to-action, while also staying within the 90-character limit.

- **Create multiple ads** - It is a good idea to create more than one ad This way when your campaign is running you can see which advertisement is the most successful and use the ones that are performing the best.

Ad Placement

It is important that you choose where you want your advertisement to be displayed. Here are the currently available options:

- The "News Feed" section of your desktop

- The "Mobile News Feed" (ads on mobile phones tend to perform the best)

- The far-right column

- Audience selection

You can define your relevant audience by selecting from the following:

- Location

- Gender

- Age

- Demographics - Demographic options include relationship status, education level, subject, school/university, undergraduate studies and workplaces.

- Interests - With interests, Facebook has developed a drop-down menu, and this is where you can target people who have liked other pages. By simply typing the page name, you can see Facebook offerings that you match.

- Connections – You can select people or groups which are already connected to your page. You can also exclude specific people.

  At the end of the process, Facebook will display how many people you will target with this configuration. For maximum coverage, you will want to match the size of your budget to the size of your audience, otherwise you won't reach everyone in your target audience. If you are targeting too few people with the interests that you have selected, then include related interests, as this will widen your reach.

Setting Up Your Budget and Campaign

Now that you have created your advertisements and selected your target audience, it is time to set your campaign budget. Your budget can be set per day or for the entire lifetime of your campaign. You can also choose to schedule your advertisement to run continuously or choose your start and end date. Next, you will select your bid price, which can be for page likes, impressions, or clicks. If you choose to bid for impressions, you will be paying every time your advertisement is seen.

Create, Capture, Convert

Anyone in business knows how valuable email addresses are, as they provide a way to contact your target market and they provide you with a perfect way to send through special offers. Facebook makes it pretty simple to create a lead capture system that will work behind the scenes.

Special Free Offer

The first step is to think of something that your target audience wants, which should be something that they consider to be of true value. This could be a short video course, a free e-book, a webinar or a special money-off coupon. Videos and webinars can be effective as they help to create an immediate personal connection with your audience. When choosing your offer, think about whether you would find it valuable and if you would be prepared to pay for it. If your answer is yes, this is probably the right offer and is likely to convince enough people to volunteer their email address.

Landing Page

The next step is to create a special landing page that contains your offer and email capture opt-in forms. You can either employ the services of a web developer or use a landing page generator service, such as www.leadpages.com or www.instapage.com. For a monthly fee, these websites offer a user-friendly service with various templates, design examples and tutorials that will help you put your landing page together. Your landing page should match your goal, which at this stage will be to visually promote your offer and to capture the email addresses of your potential customers.

Thank You Page

Your email server and most of the websites will provide you with an opportunity to create a thank you page. This page is an ideal way to offer your subscribers the chance to share your promotion with their friends.

Email Campaign

Your database of email addresses is an incredibly valuable asset. The reason that you want your audience to provide you with their details is so that you can communicate with your audience, with the aim of establishing a relationship built on trust. If you have not already set up an account with an email server, this should be your next step.

Compelling Facebook Post with Your Offer

To create your offer, you will publish a post in your News Feed by uploading an exciting image with an attention-grabbing title. Starting your post with a question can grab the attention of your audience. Then you will need to provide a comprehensive description of your offer, including why it is so valuable for your audience. Finally, you will establish a link to your landing page.

Your Audience

Selecting your audience is where Facebook excels and makes it easy for businesses to steer their campaign toward their ideal audience. Clicking on Boost Post allows your business to target demographics, interests and target fans of other pages as well.

Ready to Go

Once your system is set up, you are ready to launch your business on Facebook. It is important to monitor the results from the start of any campaign, so you can track what is effective and what isn't working at all. At this stage, you may need to adjust the message you are trying to convey, what you have on offer or your graphics until you have fine-tuned something that really works. Once your campaign is right, you have your own system where you can create, capture and convert leads into customers and your own brand advocates.

Profiting from Remarketing on Facebook

In the digital world that we live in, not only can a business connect with its target audience through content and advertising, it can also show off a product and/ or service to people who have shown an interest by visiting the business webpage but have not taken the next step of opting-in with their email or making a purchase. This is where remarketing arises as an extremely effective form of marketing.

Even with opt-in, the fact is that most people who land on your business page will disappear and never return. There could be many reasons for this, such as:

- Visitors are shopping around to find the best deals.

- They are not in a financial position to purchase at that time.

- They have not heard of your brand and are unsure about your product or service.

- They are distracted by something else which takes their focus away from your business.

- They are just not ready to make a buying decision.

Remarketing gives brands the chance to have another go at selling their products or services by showing advertisements to people who have already visited their website.

Custom Audiences

Facebook allows their advertisers to create Custom Audiences from Facebook users who have demonstrated a specific action on their website or mobile app. They set this up by adding a pixel code to their website and then by constructing and delivering advertisements based on actions that users have already taken. For example, a hotel booking website with the remarketing pixel added may be assigned to target people who have already searched for hotels but have never made a reservation. The advertiser could come up with an advertisement that offers a discount to tempt them to make a reservation.

This type of remarketing is also a perfect way to engage with users who have visited your website to sign up or opt-in.

Facebook allows businesses to create custom audiences from the email list they already have. To use these special features, just click on the tab named "Audiences" from the advertisement manager menu and select "Create a custom audience." After this, select which audience you want to target from the following and agree to the terms and conditions:

- Custom Data file audience

- Custom Mailchimp audience

- Custom audience supplied by a mobile app

- Custom audience direct from your own website

If you choose the website option, you must add the audience name and description, decide whether you want to include all your visitors to your website, or only those who have visited certain areas. Set the time the people will be saved in your audience and finally ask your developer to add the pixel code supplied by Facebook to your website.

Facebook Algorithm?

Facebook's recent algorithm makes it terribly hard for businesses to reach people without paying. Yet, don't throw up your hands in despair; there are multitudes of pages that are performing incredibly well and are receiving huge engagement without spending a penny. Obviously if you want guarantees that your posts will be viewed by a specific audience, then you have no option but to pay for it via Facebook's advertising program.

One good thing about this change is that it has cut out a lot of unwanted noise. In other words, users are only seeing what they want to see in their News Feed and are not constantly bombarded with posts that they may have no interest in. Facebook takes into consideration the posts that users engage with and will show more of these posts in their News Feed.

Here are my top tips on how you can capitalize on Facebook's algorithm:

- Make every post count.

  Create your very best content with each post you publish. Put maximum thought into how you word your posts, designing them for the highest possible engagement from your audience. Focusing on engagement and encouraging comments from your audience makes you more likely to appear on their News Feed. Avoid wasting your money, your time, and your audience's time, on frivolous posts with content that has nothing to do with your audience's needs and interests.

- Text-only posts

  Even though image posts tend to attract higher engagement, it is becoming evident that text posts are reaching more people in the News Feed. Asking questions is a fantastic way to create interest and engagement.

- Keep going, never give up.

  Many businesses simply give up and stop posting updates, which provides great opportunities for those businesses sticking with it. By staying the course and continuing to deliver quality content, you prove to your audience that you are in business for the long haul. If new people see that you are no longer posting content, they will assume that your business is no longer viable and will look elsewhere for a business that will meet their needs.

- Ask your audience to sign up.

  Let your fans know that because of Facebook's new algorithm they are unlikely to see your posts and if they wish to continue receiving your content, it is a good idea for them to sign up for your preferred list.

- Be realistic with your budget.

  Facebook is a fantastic way to provide potential customers with offers; however, you must be realistic in your spending. If you decide that Facebook advertising is a priority for you, work out what you can afford to spend and set a budget for the year.

- Promote your most valuable posts.

  Only promote the posts that have the potential to be the most popular. Check out how a post performs *before* you pay to promote it.

- Let your fans know.

  You can advertise to your fans that if they like your content and want to get your updates all the time, then they should switch on "Get Notifications." This can be found by clicking the down arrow which is situated next to the "like" button.

- Value your fans

  Never has it been so important to show your fans how much you value them in an authentic way. Be sure that if your fans have taken the time to engage in your content, engage with them by liking the comments and commenting or providing answers to any questions. This will increase the chances of a re-visit. If you are selling to businesses, then reciprocate and share their content, if it is relevant to your audience.

- Create a group.

  Creating a group around a topic which is of interest to your target audience can be a powerful way of promoting your brand and getting them to read your content or visit your blog or website.

- Instagram

  Many of your Facebook fans will also appear on Instagram. If you haven't already, this is your cue to set up your own Instagram account. It gives you yet another way to reach out to your fans. Better yet, you can post to both platforms at the same time.

Measure & Monitor Your Facebook Results

It is essential that you measure and monitor your results and performance against the goals that you have set. Measuring your results provides you with a true insight about your campaign which allows you to make changes and steer things in a different direction to reach your SMART goals and stop doing anything that is not working for you.

Once you have defined the way you intend your campaign to go, you will still have to make an estimate of how you intend to achieve these goals. With an active campaign up and running, you can easily track exactly where you are in your progress toward your original objectives. The point here is to attract feedback, as this is what it is all about and why you joined Facebook for your business in the first place. You can make your campaign work *for* you by continually measuring your success against your stated objectives and then by adjusting your tactics to achieve the results you desire.

Facebook allows you to easily track how many people have "liked" your page, the number of "likes" you have received for a post and the number of opt-in subscribers. You can also view more important and greater detailed information through the Facebook

Ads Manager, Facebook Insights, and Google Analytics. Other sites, such as Hootsuite and Buffer, provide additional analytics for Facebook.

What Are Facebook Insights?

Insights is of huge importance as it can provide you with information about how your campaign is performing and helps you to monitor and understand what is and what it not working on your page, and who is engaging with your posts. It can also assist you to make additional decisions about the best way to connect with your fans.

There are six tabs on the insight layout. These are overview, likes, reach, visits, posts and people.

Overview Tab

The overview tab shows what has been happening on your page in the previous seven days and focuses specifically on:

- Page likes – total and new

- Page reach – how many people have seen a specific post or page

- Engagement – how many different users have seen a page and possibly commented, including how they accessed your page, "likes," or comments. You will also see the previous three posts you created and can review how these have performed.

Likes Tab

The page's "Like" tab displays three metrics and shows you how your audience is growing:

- Total number of "Likes"

- Net Likes – total "Likes" minus "Unlikes"

- Where your page "Likes" came from

Clicking on this graph will show you why and how your "likes" grew on your page for any given day. This information can come from advertisements or suggested pages, pages "liked," posts by other pages, or by mobile phone. It is also possible to display multiple days.

Reach Tab

The **Post Reach** section provides the number of people that have seen your posts and how they reached them. You can click on a chart to see more information about that day or view more than one day. you can then see what posts were viewed over that time. You can see positive engagements under, **likes, comments, and shares,** along with any negative information, including whether your post was **hidden**, or a fan chose to **"unlike"** your page or mark it as **spam**.

Complete/Total Reach – This shows the number of users who have displayed interest in your page or have interacted with your posts.

Visits Tab

The **Visits** tab shows detailed information of the source of your visits.

Page and Tab Visits – This shows how many times your page was accessed.

External Referrers – This shows how frequently people came to your page from outside of Facebook.

Posts Tab

The Posts tab is divided into two separate sections:

- **When your fans are online** – This shows you the time of day that people who "like" your page are online. You can hover your mouse over a certain day and find out when your fans are most likely to see your posts.

- **Posts Types** – This shows the varied performance of your different types of posts.

- **Top Posts** – This shows which of your posts have given you the greatest engagement results.

The People Tab

Your fans –This tab displays all the information available about your fans including:

- Age

- Gender

- Geography

- Language

The age and gender chart will show how popular your page is with specific age groups compared to the total population on Facebook.

People reached, and **people engaged** – These two tabs provide a breakdown of who has viewed and interacted with your post, using the same criteria as above.

Check-ins – These are people who have recently been introduced to Facebook.

Facebook Ad Manager

Your Ad manager is where you can see at a glance how all your advertising campaigns are performing, then analyze them further to see what is not working. This is where you can view your account and billing information, see the number of post engagements, page likes, and your ad click-through rates. It is here that you can also create ad reports. By clicking the symbol you see near to top, you will then have the chance to click on **Manage Ads**. You can see comparisons between your different advertisements, how they are performing, number of clicks and the cost in your ads manager.

When advertising, it helps to create several advertisements, each with a slight variation of content, then test them for a couple days to see which one performs the best.

Facebook Ads Report

There are many reports that you can generate with Facebook ads report and you can also schedule the reports. You can set how frequently you want them created and have them sent to your email address.

Reports

It is easy to gain access to your reports. Just click on Reports and you will then be able to choose one of the following three reports:

- **General Metrics** – This report allows you to select the period you wish to view and customize the metrics so only you can see the information important to you.

- **Website Conversion** – This report allows you to see how many conversions you have received as a result of your Facebook ad. This should be done using an offsite pixel and you will also need to create your own tracking pixels on the web pages you wish to track. You can then see the specific conversions made from that page. To do this, go to your ads manager, click on power editor and the conversion tracking, which you will find on the left side column. I always give my pixel a name and select a category from the drop-down menu, then click create.

114

- **Placement Based Metrics** — This report shows the performance of your ad based on the placement of your ad and the devices your advertisement was shown on. For example, you can see the level of engagement from an ad in the News Feed from a mobile phone or on the right side of Facebook from a desktop. With this report, you can identify which device results in the highest engagement for your advertisements and place them accordingly.

To view this information, it is vital that you click Edit Columns and use the column sets to view the specific metrics you wish to see in the report.

General — This report covers all the general types of tracking, which includes the number of people you have reached, how frequently they have interacted with your page, the amount that it has cost you to make these interactions and other data such as cost per impression, cost per click, impressions, actions and the overall click-through rate.

Page — This report includes page likes, page engagement, offer claims and cost per page likes.

Offsite — This report includes all visitors who have been directed to your site, whether paid or unpaid.

App — This report includes everybody who has come through to your site using an app whether paid or unpaid.

Conversion — This report includes anybody who has converted, whether paid or unpaid.

Demographic — This report includes your ad performance by gender and age.

Geographic — This report includes your ad' performance by country.

Placement – This report shows where advertisements have been shown on Facebook, which means you can also see the performance of your advertisements against one another.

Old Reports

It is possible to also create the following old reports:

Advertising performance – This report covers statistics such as impressions, clicks, click-through rate (CTR) and the amount spent.

Responder demographics – This report provides valuable demographic information about the users who are clicking on your ads.

Actions by impression time – This report shows the number of actions organized by the impression time of the Facebook ad or sponsored story.

Inline Interactions – This report helps you to understand the engagement on page posts. It includes metrics like impressions and clicks, as well as detailed actions such as likes, photo views and video plays which have happened directly from your ads.

News Feed – This report includes statistics about impressions, clicks, click-through rate and the average position of your advertisements and sponsored stories in News Feed.

Google Analytics

If you want to track your success, it is essential that you set up a Google Analytics account. With Google Analytics, you can easily track how your campaign is performing in comparison to other social media campaigns. Google Analytics can also give you detailed information about the impact Facebook is having on your business.

Reports

Google Analytics allows you to view reports in detail, which lets you review the progress of your business. There are several different reports that can be generated such as:

Overview – As the name would suggest, this report generates an overview of where your target audience is coming from and compares all conversions resulting from social media sites.

Conversions – The conversion report is the ideal way for business owners to see how valuable the various social mediums are for their business. Google Analytics can link Facebook visits with the goals you have chosen. To do this, you will need to configure your goals in Google Analytics, which can be found under Admin and Goals. Goals in Google Analytics let you measure how often visitors take or complete a specific action, and you can either create goals from the templates offered or create your own customized goals. You will find the conversions report under the standard reporting tab under Traffic Sources, Social, then Conversions.

The Network Referral Report – This report tells you how many visitors the social networks have referred to your site and reports on the number of page visits, the total number of unique views, the duration of their visits, and approximately how many pages were viewed per visit, on average. From this information you can determine which network referred most of the traffic.

Data Activity – Data Activity provides information on how users are interacting with your website on social media sites. You can also see the URLs that have been shared and how these URLs have been shared.

Social Plug-in – The Google +1 button is tracked automatically within Google Analytics, but additional set-up is needed for Facebook. You can find the information on how to do this from the Facebook developers' site. The Social Plug-in report provides the data on which articles are shared, from which site.

Social Visitor Flow – This report shows the initial path that your visitors took from social sites, through your site, and where they left.

Landing Pages Report –This report shows the engagement metrics for each URL. These include page views, average length of visit, and the pages that were viewed during the visit.

Trackbacks Report – The Trackbacks report shows which sites are linked with your content and how many visits those sites are sending to you. This is an effective way for you to work out what kind of content is most successful so that you can create similar content while also building relationships with those who are consistently linking to your content.

Google Analytics and Your Custom Campaigns

With Google analytics, you can create URLs for custom campaigns for website tracking. This will set you up to identify which content drives the most visitors to your landing pages and website. If you want to know which Facebook posts are sending the most traffic or which links in an email or in banners are sending you the most traffic. Custom campaigns let you to measure this and see what works most effectively, as they let you add parameters to your URL.

Using the URL builder

Type "URL builder" into Google and click on the first result.

Tip: The URL builder form will only appear if you are signed into Google.

Add the URL you plan to track, complete it, and click the "Submit" button. Next, customize the URL, following the instructions given in a previous chapter. Once you have everything set up, you can track the results using Google Analytics.

Chapter 10: Building A Powerful Brand with Facebook

As a business, your main aim through the entire process of building your Facebook business page is to connect with and convert prospects into customers through your blog, website, Facebook or other social media networks. This requires you to master the following:

- Connect: Your product must be the connection between your prospect and what it is they need; therefore, the first thing you must do is connect the two. To do this, you must identify who your prospects are and then connect with them by offering something they need or want.

- Capture: Now that you have found your audience, you want to capture them in a way that will allow you to establish and continue your relationship with them, either by email or other ways you communicate your brand message. It is at this point that you should think about offering an incentive, so you can capture the names and email details of your prospective customers.

- Convert: Now that you have captured your prospects, you will be looking to convert them into paying customers by continuing to build and nurture your relationship. This is where and when you will want to offer them content via email or another type of social media platform to tempt them to sign up for an exclusive or unique offer.

Defining Your Brand

To successfully achieve this, your brand needs to be well-defined and it needs to be communicated to the end user through everything you do or say whether on Facebook, your website, blog or another platform. Your brand is the most important attribute of your business whether you are a sole trader or a huge organization, and it is your brand that you want prospects and customers to trust, respect and ultimately fall in love with enough to purchase and continue to purchase your product or service for years to come.

It is your brand that makes your business different from all other businesses. With the digital age we live in, it is so important to nurture and grow your brand, building awareness and a target audience through social media, particularly Facebook.

There has never been a better time to build your brand and communicate its message to a target audience than now and by using Facebook. The main ingredient for your success is your brand, and Facebook provides you with the channel to communicate it. Facebook has made it possible to communicate with your target audience daily. Get this right; connect the right brand experience and target the right audience and you cannot fail.

Whether you already have an established brand, are in the middle of creating your brand, or are putting the finishing touches to it, you need to understand that your brand will underpin your entire campaign on your Facebook business page. Therefore, your brand must be strong, clear, consistent and well-defined. Once you have your brand established, your business must go on to create it, communicate it, picture it, display it, speak it, promote it and be true to it.

In this last chapter we are going to end by looking at everything you need to define and create your brand and make sure that it gets right into the hearts of your target audience.

The word "brand" can be defined in many ways. I view a brand as a model that incorporates all the necessary information about your business. Your brand is more than a symbol or a logo. It represents your character, your values, and your personality, all bundled up into a tiny package that you set before your potential customers. It encompasses the promise of all you stand for and the goodness of all the products you stand behind. Your brand identifies you as separate from the competition, in a good way.

Why is branding so important? Branding, your presence before the public, helps you and your business to grow and thrive. Over time, as you interact with people and build a positive reputation, you will become a memorable entity represented by your brand presentations. But first you must do the work of forging those relationships, person by person, purchase by purchase, through consistent actions communicating what you stand for to your customers

A strong brand has several benefits. It encourages customer loyalty. It also invites trust by the reputation of your good name. These two things alone can boost your sales.

You can do this through your Facebook business page, as this will give you the opportunity to truly understand your customers, which in turn will encourage them to choose your product or service and become repeat customers. Before you begin to launch any marketing activities, you require a concise understanding of your brand.

For this, you need to truly understand both who you are as a business and who will be most interested in your products or services. When you are in the position to begin defining your target audience, you need to know which of your products, if you are offering more than one, is the most popular and the most profitable. This is where you will focus your efforts to find and connect with the best possible audience and create the ultimate brand experience.

Conclusion

Now that we have come to the end, you should feel excited about all the steps, techniques and strategies presented here that you can use to crush it in Facebook! Don't try to do everything at once. Just focus on one thing at a time and get it done to the best of your ability and then move on to the next thing. Over time, you will find it easy to put systems in place that make it easy for you to maintain your page while it still produces incredible results.

However, what is it going to take for your business to make more of an impression than its competitors? If you are now following or have ever followed any brands, you will have seen that there are brands and businesses that do stand out from all the rest. These businesses and brands are those that appear far bigger than their actual products. They have a large, highly targeted audience, the best content, the most interaction and engagement, and have no fear about posting viral content. They appear to truly understand their audiences, and in return their audiences hang on their every word.

These outstanding businesses are known as "Social Media Superstars" and as such, they know exactly how to harness and use the power of social media for their own gain and the gain of their business.

Let's recap the information and steps you need to implement to make your business better than any of your competitors who are using Facebook marketing. You need to focus on your audience and understand that while they are vital, there are a few other things that you also need to remember. The reason your competitors are so good with social media marketing is *not* because they have some type of super powers; it is not chance or coincidence either. It is because they know and understand that their success is all down to their audience and how they communicate their message to that audience.

Your main aim is to succeed in your business. However, to do this you must build everything around your audience and what they want. By giving them what they want, you will build and ultimately establish a solid and valuable fan base who will eventually buy your products. These people will become your brand ambassadors and will do a lot of the demanding work for you. Loyal customers can be counted on to tell others about the products they like, sharing content you have posted, thereby harnessing the most effective form of marketing you could never buy: word-of-mouth advertising.

To achieve this and to stand out, you need to remember the following:

- Commit fully to your campaign and to working your business for the long run.

- Believe completely in what you offer, whether it's a product or a service, and always do it to the best of your ability.

- Make everything revolve around your audience and their needs.

- Offer incredible value, free advice, and accurate information.

It all boils down to your targeted audience, what they need, and what they want, and the best way for you to provide it.

I hope that you have enjoyed my book and found it valuable, so much so that you will continue to use it as your handbook for success as you manage your own Facebook business page. It is true that the social media universe continues to change, but once you have mastered your basic techniques, you will find it very easy to keep abreast of any types of change.

In conclusion, I thank you again for taking time out of your busy schedule to read this book and for committing to use my strategies and tactics to help your business grow. All that is left for me is to wish you all the best things for you and your business. Go ahead and take action right now. Choose the most important thing you could be doing to make your page better and get started. Be smart and persistent and you are bound to be successful.

Thanks for reading.

If this book has helped you or someone you know then I invite you to leave a nice review right now; it would be greatly appreciated.

My Other Books

For more great knowledge of the world, be sure to check out my other books and author page at:

USA: https://www.amazon.com/author/susanhollister

UK: http://amzn.to/2qiEzA9

Or simply type my name into the search bar: Susan Hollister

Thank You

Made in the USA
Lexington, KY
21 April 2019